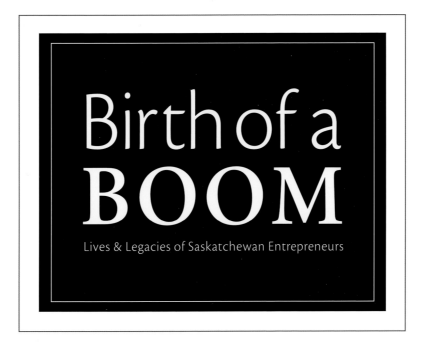

Birth of a BOOM

Lives & Legacies of Saskatchewan Entrepreneurs

SUZANNE PASCHALL

with a foreword by W. Brett Wilson

May 13/12
To a special friend
Edward Staub
from Casimir & Maria Broda
(pro. of Broda Construction Inc.)
Jan. 6 - Mar. 28 - 2004

Prairie
Policy Centre

Executive Director, Prairie Policy Centre: Allan Evans
Communications Manager, Prairie Policy Centre: Laurel Reich
Photography and photo editing: Debra Marshall (www.debramarshall.ca)
Design: Jacqueline Germin (www.jgermin.com)
Editor: Pam Bustin
Indexer: Ursula Acton

Published by Prairie Policy Centre
2229 Avenue C North
Saskatoon, SK, Canada   S7L 5Z2
T 306.242.2981 F: 306.242.1329
info@prairiecentre.com
www.prairiecentre.com

Printed in Canada by Friesens Book Division

First edition: November, 2009

ISBN 978-0-9730456-2-8

Library and Archives Canada Cataloguing in Publication

Paschall, Suzanne, 1958–
Birth of a boom: lives & legacies of Saskatchewan
entrepreneurs/Suzanne Paschall; with a foreword by W. Brett Wilson.

Includes bibliographical references and index.
ISBN 978-0-9730456-2-8 (bound).–ISBN 978-0-9730456-3-5 (pbk.)

1. Entrepreneurship–Saskatchewan.
2. Businesspeople–Saskatchewan–Biography.
3. Saskatchewan–Economic conditions–1991-. I. Prairie Policy Centre II. Title.

HC117.S3P38 2009   338.092'27124   C2009-906183-X

For Norm Wallace, whose passion for a free and prosperous Saskatchewan inspires us all.

To my father, who showed me that integrity, loyalty and hard work are
the most important traits of successful business people and who made me believe
I could achieve any goal, if only I wanted it badly enough.

W. Brett Wilson
Foreword

I am delighted to lend my support to a book project about entrepreneurship in Saskatchewan–two subjects near and dear to my heart. Like many people from Saskatchewan, I have a soft spot for home. I'm an unapologetic prairie boy. I have great respect for my prairie heritage, and the innovative people who pioneered our province.

One of those early pioneers was my great-grandfather, a man named Benjamin Prince. He was my father's grandfather. Benjamin was born in the East, and came west with his brother. He eventually settled in Battleford, and built the first sawmill there, and later, the first flour mill. The original diversified investor, he also opened a department store, and was an active farmer and rancher. Benjamin was also a great political leader. He represented Battleford in the Legislative Assembly of the Northwest Territories. He later became mayor of Battleford, and was eventually appointed to the Senate.

Although I didn't know him personally, Benjamin was a great source of encouragement for me as an entrepreneur. I have a strong psychological attachment to him, and have sought to follow his lead as a community builder.

One of Saskatchewan's greatest assets has always been its people. There is something about growing up here–in a land that is as harsh as it is beautiful–that has helped create some of the finest people in the world–people who are resourceful, respected, and solid to the core–part of a special breed.

What occurred in Saskatchewan in the late 1800s and early 1900s is a great example of entrepreneurial spirit. In a relatively short time, determined settlers turned the wild prairie into one of the most prosperous agricultural economies in the world.

Today, we're seeing a new kind of entrepreneur, turning knowledge, technology, and innovation into new products and services that are the foundation of the new global economy.

Of all the things I've learned in my business journey, it's that entrepreneurship is about finding innovative solutions to old problems and taking calculated risks to bring those ideas to market. Many of the stories you will read in this book bring to life the ups and downs, risks and rewards of one of the greatest endeavours on earth–entrepreneurship–and the colourful characters who were inspired to try something new.

One of my first entrepreneurial adventures happened when I was still a student at the University of Saskatchewan. Because many of our school dances were held off campus, my friend Daryl Rudichuk and I saw an opportunity to make some money by offering students rides to and from the events. We rented two buses at $50 each for the night and charged each student $1 per round trip. Since a cab ride was $5 for the same trip, we attracted hundreds of customers. The bus shuttle was so successful that we ran our business several more times that year– earning hundreds of dollars each time–when most of our friends were earning $2.25 an hour in minimum wage jobs. Our company was so profitable that we could afford to take cabs to and from the dances rather than ride on the buses!

A lot of time has passed since that first attempt at running my own business, and I've had some successes–and a few failures–along the way. But I've never lost my passion for entrepreneurship, and for inspiring others to experience the joys and benefits of building community by building businesses.

Not long ago, the opportunity came for me to connect my love of entrepreneurship with my passion for philanthropy. I made a $1 million gift to the University of Saskatchewan to establish The Wilson Centre for Entrepreneurial Excellence. When we were in the planning stages of The Wilson Centre,

we purposely developed it as a multi-disciplinary centre that would transcend servicing just the school of business, which is what most people associate with entrepreneurship.

The Wilson Centre has a vision for becoming one of the pre-eminent centres for entrepreneurship in Canada. With an economic, environmental and social consciousness, the Centre's mandate is to inspire entrepreneurship and innovation among young people in all college disciplines, and to connect business leaders, researchers and potential financiers with investment opportunities focused on Western Canada.

It is my hope that these initiatives–along with this book published by the Prairie Policy Centre –will inspire a new generation of entrepreneurs who will create another wave of wealth and prosperity for the prairies.

Acknowledgments

I have been asked if this book was commissioned or independent, and I have, truthfully and happily, been able to respond, "both." Though the entire creative team was paid to produce a book on this topic, our benefactor and publisher (the Prairie Policy Centre) exerted no pressure or preference in the development of the content, other than to hire us based on our vision of how such a work might look and feel; and to present us with the 13 subjects their board selected, based on criteria they believe is important. Being paid allowed me to take the last year to focus my efforts exclusively on this project, a rarity in the world of a freelance writer.

Support

This relationship between author and publisher has been much appreciated. I need to single out three very important individuals in this regard. First, to one of those board members and the man who personifies the word "entrepreneur," I owe a debt of gratitude to Norm Wallace. Without his original vision and his unwavering faith in me and the creative team, this book would not have been possible, let alone been the wonderful journey it has been. To Executive Director Al Evans, I extend my heartfelt thanks for his staunch support and his unerring judgment in recognizing that to over-manage this project would be to kill its spirit and freedom. To Communications Manager Laurel Reich, I am grateful for the emotional support, her intelligent reader's eye and her astute knowledge of the Saskatchewan business landscape.

And, of course, if Norm's vision had not been shared by the PPC board and Chairman Dean Gagne, the idea would have died at the board room table. The board's book committee, also chaired by Dean, has been supportive and enthusiastic, believing totally in the importance of telling these stories.

This project has been an unusual hybrid in the publishing world–neither a corporate commission, nor a book following the traditional path of author-presented-to-publisher. I competed with other writers for the opportunity to do this "job," and it has turned into anything but a job. Like the entrepreneurs in this book, I found myself in love with the work, so much so that no hours were counted, no overtime recorded. The same is true of my compatriots in the production process.

Teamwork

This is my first book, and I have learned through conversation with much more experienced published authors that the opportunity for an author to choose a book's designer, photographer and editor is rare. When presented with this task, I had no trouble in selecting my team. I pay tribute to the talents of designer Jacqueline Germin and photographer Debra Marshall, and even more to their willingness to take this journey with me. To my editor Pam Bustin, many thanks for your willingness to step out of your genre and apply your keen sense of story, character, plot and action to this manuscript, and for understanding why that's the kind of editor I so wanted.

Together we made this book with a unique collaborative approach that, while at times was challenging and frustrating, in the end, was one of the most uplifting and significant team experiences of my career. I hope, and believe, they feel the same way. This became *our* book; not *my* book, and I think it shows…in every bit of graphic design nuance slaved over by Jacqueline, and emanating from every feature photo shot carefully created by Debra. Though invisible in the final product, you will sense the careful attention to story detail and structure that is the result of Pam's crafting. Please savour these elements along with the reading of the stories. Our working philosophy was that it takes all elements combined in perfect balance to best tell these stories; and to both show our pride in the 'product,' and our respect for these people whose life-long entrepreneurial successes give us all so much inspiration.

Partnership

I would also like to thank the many supporters of this unique enterprise. Yet another unusual aspect of this project is that the book was produced entirely by private sector contributions. These various individuals and organizations stepped up eagerly to fund what is not an inexpensive undertaking. This also includes, notably, the Wilson Centre for Entrepreneurial Excellence at the University of Saskatchewan, whose board also believes in the book's potential to educate, inspire and engage young people within whom the fire of enterprise smoulders. Specifically, my heartfelt thanks to Wilson Centre Director Sanj Singh; and to the Centre's namesake, Brett Wilson, for graciously agreeing to provide an illuminating foreword.

The heroes

Finally, my humble thanks to the subjects of this book. Your lives and legacies have forever changed our prairie landscape, and we owe you for what you, and your forebears, have accomplished in the building of prosperity in our province. Your spirit, your honesty, and your humility are etched in my memory: you are my heroes. To your families, who have been so generous with their time, stories and treasured family photographic material, we all thank you. And, to the employees and colleagues and others who have contributed their thoughts, we are also grateful for your role in saying what the subjects were often too modest to say about themselves, but which clearly needed to be said.

One last, important, note: As every subject reminded me, where there are these 13 stories, look across the street, or in the next town over, and you will find, literally, hundreds more like them.

One thing we know is that Saskatchewan breeds entrepreneurs. Hopefully their stories will someday be told as well. They are all part of our enterprising heritage.

My heroes

Finally, to Lucy, Tom and Sarah…for helping me find my inner harmony in this most challenging year, and for giving the best you had when it was needed the most, Nakummemarialuk.

CONTENTS

Contents

Birth of a Boom
Pride of place

My father has the soul of an entrepreneur. Though he worked for entrepreneurs his entire career, he also had his own businesses…a large kennel operation (half of the sales of which were to Canadians); a salad dressing manufacturing business, and partnership in oil exploration. My mother was a full partner in some of these ventures, and also ran a pre-school out of our home.

As I listened to the tales of the business leaders in this book, I heard familiar echoes of my parents' story– and those of their forebears.

Though my prairie heritage wasn't in Saskatchewan, it might as well have been. My dad, Herb, was born to a family of nine children on July 3, 1919, on a farm in mid-western Kansas. His parents were German hard red winter wheat farmers who had emigrated from Russia at the turn of the century, as were many who came to Saskatchewan.

My grandpa had been ill in the early '20s, and couldn't run their farm, so the family moved into the small town of Otis, where he started the Freidenberger Creamery for Fairmont Foods. But as the family grew and the Depression descended, they needed more money to survive. They moved back out to a leased farm, and my grandma, Sophie, and Dad and his siblings worked the farm. Cash for gasoline and food was provided by selling eggs and cream.

At age 17, my father started sacking potatoes in the dark basement of a small grocery store. It was the first in a regional, family-owned chain that would become J.S. Dillon & Sons. He would retire 42 years later as vice president and controller of the 30,000-employee company, now a division of the Kroger Company. Throughout his career, he and my mother continued to build various entrepreneurial ventures on the side.

And so, I realize, like many in this book, entrepreneurism is also in *my* blood.

There's an intensity within our prairie sky–whether it's the spectacular shifting hues of a Northern lights display, the dark colours of an approaching storm, or, as here, the painted kaleidoscope of a Northern sunset. To Saskatchewan entrepreneurs it's a symbol of inspiration. "The sky," says Joe Bloski, "is the limit."

Prairie entrepreneur stories transcend national borders.
The author's grandparents, George and Sophie, display a sign
from their 1930s Kansas creamery business.

The boom heard across Canada

The news over the past few years announcing that
Saskatchewan was, finally, a "have" province probably
surprised a lot of people. The "Saskaboom" reverber-
ated across the country in 2008 by way of the media, and
news announcers sounded as though they couldn't quite
believe what they were reading on their teleprompters.
"Apparently…" they said, "Saskatchewan is experiencing an economic upswing and outperforming the rest of
Canada by nearly every measure."

Who knew? Actually, there were some who were
less surprised–those who had been watching small[1]
and medium-sized businesses grow and prosper…
slowly, but steadily. Not over years, but across decades.
The groundwork for much of the stability and prosperity in today's province is not only the result of a rich
resource base: It's also a result of people figuring out
how to get at it, how to maximize it, and how to
diversify from it. That's what entrepreneurs do, and
they began doing it here at the turn of the 20th century.

It started small. Many of the large businesses
in the province are a product of local home-grown
entrepreneurship. Of the 130 largest private manufacturers in Saskatchewan, 50% were originally
started by an entrepreneur as a local small business
venture.[2] Small businesses still power our economy.
They contribute more than $3.3 billion annually to
Saskatchewan's economy.[3] They represent 96% of
all firms in the province, directly employing about
one third of Saskatchewan's labour force (more than
140,000 people) and accounting for 42% of total
private sector employment.[4]

The prairie entrepreneur

As it turns out, many of Saskatchewan's entrepreneurs are the progeny of ancestors who needed to be
smart, inventive, and think ahead just to survive.
They were immigrants who started with nothing.
They modelled a strong work ethic, and were fiscally
aware. They understood moderate, calculated risk.
They were creative problem-solvers, and as focused
on their goals as a speeding arrow. Their children
watched, and learned.

The prairie created its *own* lessons. These people
were both nurtured by their parents, and "natured"
by the often harsh, unyielding environment that still
challenges us…a frigid winter; a resistant, stone-
littered field; the threatening turbulence of a storm.
The prairie teaches us patience, persistence, meeting
challenge, and succeeding with teamwork.

Nobody needs to teach these entrepreneurs
about hard work. They arose at 4 a.m. each school
day to get their chores in–before they ate breakfast,
before the sun rose, before any city kid even thought
about waking up.

The author's father Herb and sister Alma at harvest in the 1930s.

A breed apart

Prairie breeding creates a certain kind of entrepreneur. A balance between family and business is important, and the values of the former infuse the culture of the latter. As Chapter 13's Gord Broda, of Broda Construction, says, "Growing up in Saskatchewan kept us grounded. Saskatchewan business people have stayed very level headed–even with today's recession, Saskatchewan hasn't been in any real trouble.

"We're not 'boom or bust' kind of people. We're 'steady as she goes' kind of people. Nobody here gets in trouble by leveraging with an enormous amount of debt. We've all been raised in that environment…you balance hard work with commitment to family–it's a pretty good recipe for success."

The history of starting with nothing but a strong desire and a wide-open prairie sky is also common to prairie entrepreneurs' background, as Chapter 4's Joe Bloski identifies. "Our forebears came from small, or no, beginnings. They came to this country with nothing.

"People in cities look out and can't see or think beyond the wall of skyscrapers. Here, you look out to the distant horizon…the sky really *is* the limit. I think there's a real difference in philosophy about what is *possible*. And that certainly is a valuable characteristic for an entrepreneur to have."

The lessons from the land are strong metaphors for entrepreneurism, as Chapter 5's Gavin Semple describes. "That's Saskatchewan: It represents the life of a lot of successful companies around here. We've all had the same kind of upbringing and history. Because of it, you learn to relate seeding to harvest; you see it live from the time you're little. And you learn quickly that when you work hard, you *will* get a result at the end of the process."

The country recently saw one of those results quantified in the Canadian Federation of Independent Business' 2009 ranking of Canada's most entrepreneurial cities, where Saskatchewan dominated, taking five out of the 10 top places–Saskatoon in the top spot, accompanied by Moose Jaw (#4), Lloydminster (#5), Regina (#8) and Prince Albert (#10).[5]

As you will discover in these pages, though Saskatchewan's boom may have just recently sounded, it has been rumbling, quietly, like the muffled thunder of an approaching herd, for much longer.

Herb (2nd from left) poses outside his one-room Kansas schoolhouse in the late 1920s.

Norm Wallace
Roots of a renegade

As a 19-year-old immigrant from Tipperary County, Ireland, in 1957, Norman Wallace landed in Vancouver looking for what he and his pals had been promised by the Canadian government–work aplenty. But what they found was just the opposite–no work, and especially no work for anyone tagged with the label "immigrant."

One Sunday, after searching endlessly the previous week for a job–any job, he returned to his boarding house room and broke down in tears. The next day, while walking down Denman Street in Stanley Park, he finally saw a sign in front of a bank that said, "Tellers needed." He went to the head office on Granville Street, sweated through, and passed, a 100-question written test, and then the manager asked to see his grade 12 completion certificate, a requirement for the position. Having only completed grade 8, the penniless and hungry Norm desperately searched his mind for a solution. Missing out on this job was *not* an option.

"I don't have the certificate with me," he said.

"Well bring it in, and the job is yours," the manager replied.

Norm returned to his room, thinking he might be beaten. Then, he remembered something. He rushed back to the bank office with a piece of paper and handed it to the manager. "It's in Gaelic," Norm said. "Let me translate it." He read off an official-sounding bit of text indicating that he had completed grade 12.

In actual fact, the beautiful scrawling calligraphy acknowledged his proficiency in swimming, not school. But the bit of blarney did the trick, and Norm Wallace had his first job in Canada.

Norm Wallace, recalling his early days as an Irish immigrant to Canada, staunchly remains "beholden to nobody."

Clohinch House, Norm's childhood home. Originally homesteaded in the 1700s by the Sifton family who immigrated to Canada to become giants in the food industry. The Wallaces bought the home in 1780. It still stands in Templederry, County Tipperary, Ireland.

Early lessons:
learning from strong, proud women

This experience, and others like it in the following years, helped shape the young immigrant into one of Saskatchewan's and Canada's most colourful, controversial and successful entrepreneurs.

"Oh yes, we were poor," Norm says. "Dirt poor." He describes difficulties growing up in Tipperary in a family of five with a father who, as he puts it, "wasn't the most responsible" supporter of his large and needy family. As his father's unhappiness grew, he turned to gambling–making Norm's mother's struggle to run the family grocery store even tougher.

It was the women of the family who were the greatest influence on Norm, and he attributes much of his toughness of character to them. "My mother was a Mooney, and they were very strong, proud women," Norm says. "She was a character and a real 'people person,' but she never had an education." The toughest of them all was his grandmother, Annie Mooney (from the family of Canadian women's

rights activist, Nellie Mooney McClung). She ran the family farm, and was involved in the Protestant church (a small minority in the nearly all-Catholic area). Norm visited her often, sitting at the fireside listening to her recite old-fashioned sayings. "I especially remember one," Norm recalls, "that went, 'Put a beggar on horseback and he'll ride you to hell.'" From these no-nonsense women, the young Norm learned that life was not easy, and that hard work was the only way to survive–let alone thrive.

Though he was a hardy boy, Norm did have an incident that ultimately held some historical medical significance. While at his grandmother's, he had a bicycle accident that caused a deadly bacterial infection in his leg known as osteomyelitis; a disease of the bone that, at the time, often required amputation of the affected limbs. He spent six months in hospital and became one of the first people in the British Isles to be given a new drug called penicillin, which saved his leg.

At age 12, Norm was sent to a Dublin boarding school, where he describes abuses that paralleled those experienced by Canada's native population in the residential school system. "I said 'no,' and got away with it," he says. Others around him weren't so fortunate. As soon as they could, he and his friends escaped to other parts of the world–one to Africa, a brother to Rhodesia and Norm to Canada.

"We give you a rope…"

"In those days, it was dead easy to immigrate to Canada," Norm says. "Not like today." After six months at the bank in Vancouver, he heard from a friend that there were jobs selling roofing and siding in Saskatchewan, so he moved to Regina. He found the prairie folks he encountered in his door-to-door sales work to be "very nice."

Later, he moved to Winnipeg, where he lived at the YMCA, and had a job with National Cash Register (NCR). But soon he found a challenge that would keep him occupied for a number of years. "I went to apply for a job at Winnipeg Supply and Fuel and the manager said, 'We want you to go manage a branch in Saskatoon for us,'" he recalls. "Well, I didn't know anything about building products, or branches, but the fellow said, 'Look, we have a way of doing things here. We give you a rope, and then find out if you hang yourself, or not.'"

Norm went to Saskatoon. He remained at Winnipeg Supply and Fuel for 15 years, and learned a *lot* about managing…and building products. This experience would set him up for his next step– running his own business.

Now with a wife, Agnes, a public health nurse, and two young sons to support, Norm felt the need to build more than just an income. He wanted to build a future for his family. But it wasn't going to come easily.

"We wanted to farm, and we found a perfect place owned by an old Norwegian near Outlook. He had friends who recommended us to buy it," Norm says. "But he was eccentric, and didn't want to sell to us because we were immigrants."

Dejected, Norm and Agnes thought about returning to Ireland, but just didn't feel it was the right time. That's when they hit on the idea of starting their own business. With $4,000 painstakingly saved from several years of Agnes' work and Norm's multiple jobs (which included cleaning stores for Pinder's Drugs and managing an apartment building on Main Street, in addition to his management job at Winnipeg Supply and Fuel), they opened Wallace Construction in 1972, at the Diamond Industrial Centre on 33rd Street with $100,000 in inventory.

Then, within six months, he opened the Regina branch. "He barely had Saskatoon up and running when he opened Regina," Wallace Controller Dale Boothman says. "He had lots of ambition." Norm's faith in the Regina branch and its staff would be well rewarded in the future, but there was no way to know that at the time. It was the kind of early expansion that has felled more than one business in the start-up stage.

"We risked everything we had," Norm says. "It was go-for-broke. Canadians are very comfortable and used to getting supported by their government. That wasn't our experience growing up in Ireland, so we didn't expect hand-outs. We just worked."

Twenty seven-year-old Norm with his new bride, Agnes, on their way from the ceremony at St. John's Anglican Cathedral to the reception on February 20, 1965.

The fiery and passionate business owner soon got embroiled in his first issue (a lawsuit) within six months, but when that was resolved in the company's favour, he moved on. Within a few years, he'd developed a small but highly capable and loyal staff.

Though tough and opinionated, Norm turned out to be a great boss. Says Dale, one of his earliest and longest serving employees of 33 years, "He's very generous and loyal to his employees. There are a number of people who've been with him for 20 to 25 years. He lets employees do their own thing. He's very trusting of people working for him."

James Waldbillig, branch manager with 22 years at Wallace, agrees, adding that Norm really appreciates the hard work and loyalty of his staff. "Even now, though he's 'semi-retired,' Norm's in every morning. And he notices things. He'll say, 'Man, the boys in the warehouse are really working hard. I've seen five trucks come in today!' He's not a big back-slapper, but when he does say something he means it."

Of the early lawsuit situations, the two men say Norm handled them extremely well, and it ended up establishing a reputation for the company that was to be beneficial. "He was pretty small starting out–he would always fight for what he thought," James says. "When the main suppliers threatened to cut their lines, he stuck to his principles. If he thought he was right, he wasn't afraid to spend dollars to prove it."

Both say they learned the value of sticking to principles, and being choosey about who you work with in all areas of business. Steering away from bad situations can bring about growth. "At the end of the day, it was a very good thing for Norm to do," Dale says. "It opened up things we would've never done otherwise."

When the North American manufacturers refused to sell to Wallace, they started importing from overseas. "We wouldn't have done that otherwise," James says. "Today, for a small company like us, we import a lot, and it's very profitable. And, in a recession like we have now, we're a small company, but we're not hurting as much because our suppliers are elsewhere," James adds.

Now the company is so diversified in its supply lines that no one problem causes them pain for any length of time. It has created a great stability and reliability that they pass on to their customers.

"Tough sells"...new ideas

When an employee came to him and asked why they didn't get bonuses when there was a good year, Norm said, "Good idea!" He implemented a profit-sharing plan for staff and, recognizing the value of content employees, created empowerment by essentially turning over the business decisions to them.

Wallace Construction became known for being a "renegade" in the construction industry, by launching new ideas gleaned from international travel and

Rolling out the roofing membrane, another revolutionary product carried by Wallace, for a new Saskatoon Wal-Mart, in 2009.

Norm annually hosts 2,000 stakeholders at casual Saskatoon and Regina customer appreciation barbecue events, affectionately known as "Wally Days."

Norm's constant search for new and better ways to do things. "We brought steel studs to Saskatchewan," Norm says. "Boy, that was a tough sell. But now they're being used." That product was actually developed at his previous employer, Winnipeg Supply and Fuel. "Steel is cheaper than wood, the walls are straight, it goes up faster, and can be shipped in smaller packages," he says.

Other innovations included developing an egg-crate like cardboard product (called the Wallace Void Form) that, when fitted between soil and a cement floor, keeps the cement from cracking. The cardboard eventually collapses, leaving the soil six inches lower than the floor, so the cement surface isn't affected when the soil shifts and settles.

Another innovative product was a blanket for insulating pipes in the cold Northern oil fields, which was inexpensive, lightweight and easy to ship.

Being aggressive in the construction industry is a necessity, not a "nice to do," James says. "Being aggressive and smart, and physical, in construction is important. You need to be quick-witted." Aggressiveness translates directly to marketing and sales, which is James' forté. "If you phone me and you're looking for something, and I just say, 'we got it,' and I quit, don't do add-on selling, I've lost an opportunity. I need to ask 'Do you need roof membrane–what about insulation?' Or just simple follow-ups: 'Am I getting this order, yes or no?'"

Norm has taught his staff many things about business, much from examples of him exercising his principles and down-to-earth philosophies. "I learned not to take too much grief from people," James says.

Beholden to nobody

Today, Wallace Construction employs some 35 people in Saskatoon and Regina; has export experience in Ukraine, Mexico, China, Japan, the United Kingdom and the United States, and lists annual sales in excess of $20 million. Seventy construction product lines in 36 categories are distributed for more than 80 suppliers from Canada, the U.S. China, Mexico, Germany, France, Belgium and, more recently, Ireland and Japan.

And the quality of the staff is "second to none," says Dale. "You talk to anyone in the industry, Wallace provides knowledgeable, technically astute people. People trust the advice when they come to us." James adds, "We have some of the smartest people in Western Canada no, I'd say Canada, at what they do."

This high-quality, empowered and action-oriented staff freed up some of Norm's time, which he quickly used to branch out into other business interest areas, including taking on a partnership of an international asset tracing firm out of Ireland. The tough-talking, no-holds-barred Irish Canadian became known for saying what was on his mind, but also for an ability to look into the future and see what needed to change. That attracted the attention of a variety of industry companies who wanted his advice. In the past 30 years, he's sat on numerous boards, including oil giant Enterra (Calgary), BCIC Investments, SED Systems and the Saskatoon Construction Association. Along the way, he also helped found the Provincial Exporters Association, the Canadian Taxpayers Federation and the Prairie Policy Centre.

Never one to be concerned about people's opinion of him ("I don't care if people think I'm a nut case," he says. "I'm beholden to nobody."), Norm continued challenging systems he considered to be faulty, including both provincial and federal governments. In 2003, he was asked to give evidence to the Federal Standing Committee on Citizenship and Immigration, where he pointed the finger at both provincial and federal policies and practices that he felt either deterred the healthy flow of immigration to Canada, or disadvantaged immigrants who did make it into the country. Having had the immigrant experience made his contribution compelling and credible. Committee chair Joe Fontana said, "Thanks to you for an absolutely fantastic glimpse of the vision you have for your province."[1]

It's that vision of how much better things could be, the same view he held as a young man immigrating to a new country, that seems to be the driving motivation for Norm—in business, politics and in how he views his community and his role in it. In hindsight, the predictions he made in 2003 about growth in Saskatchewan due to better use of resources, have proven to be visionary. Saskatchewan's development of resource-based and related industries has been part of the engine for the recent and much-heralded economic boom in the province.

Coming together in crisis

Family and community are very important to Norm, and one particularly painful experience was the catalyst to a deepened understanding and appreciation of his community. On April 8, 1996, the Ontario Street office building of Wallace Construction burned to the ground. Norm was out of town at the time. When he was called with the news, he didn't go back for three days. "I didn't want to see the ashes," he says, and tears well up in his eyes, some 12 years later. "Everything Agnes and I had worked for was gone. People think there was no loss because of insurance coverage, but the value of the loss was three times what we had for coverage. We had $1 million in insurance, but we lost $3 million."

Out of those ashes, came amazing examples of community support. Though all records of receivables were destroyed in the fire (including personal mementos Norm had collected over the years), Wallace recovered 99% of what they were owed. Customers

10   **The Wallace Construction fire on April 8, 1996 devastated Norm's family and staff.**

Inferno on 41st

Two north-end businesses levelled by fire

By Betty Ann Adam
of The StarPhoenix

On Friday morning, radio news reminded Anton Schouten about the tragic explosion in Oklahoma City one year ago.

By 6 p.m. a raging fire had left his own thriving cardboard box business a mass of rubble.

Fortunately, in this case, there was no human tragedy as the four employees inside Consolidated Packaging managed to escape after an explosion rocked the adjacent Wallace Construction.

All of the Wallace employees — the fire department was told there were nine working — also escaped injury.

Consolidated Packaging's new, 100,000-square-foot plant on 41st Street East burned to the ground Friday afternoon along with Wallace Construction.

"The building is ruined. Everything is gone," Schouten said in a telephone interview.

—Photo by Larry L[...]

It's a losing battle Friday for firefighters trying to control the raging fire

Their efforts saved two adjacent commercial properties from fire damage, although the businesses sustained smoke and heat damage.

Although police on the scene [...]

from Wallace Construction in two different places. Then some guys ran past (the building) and then it blew. The (north) wall just blew right out," Deptuck said extending his arms wide. [...]

selling wooden pallets.

Schouten estimates an insured [...] of $250,000 to $300,000.

He is relieved that he takes [...] ly precaution of making a c[...]

Though, thankfully, no one was injured in the 1996 Wallace Construction fire, it destroyed many of Norm's personal mementos, and $3 million in inventory. Insurance only covered one third of that inventory value.

voluntarily called, saying, "I don't even know what I owe you, but I'm sending you $10,000." Forklifts and workers came from neighbouring companies, volunteering to help in reconstruction of the building. And, despite a strike at the time, SaskTel rerouted the firm's Saskatoon phone lines to Wallace's Regina branch, and customers were being supplied with overnight service.

"We were up and running in two days," Dale remembers. "The support we managed to get from our staff, both in Regina and Saskatoon, was amazing. The fire was on Friday, and we were servicing customers with orders on Monday."

Regina branch manager at the time, Del Hamerlindl, was a hero, Norm says. Regina took orders, and shipped them to Saskatoon for delivery, so there was no down-time for customers. "Del's been with us since Wallace started, and he's respected as one of the best representatives of the construction supply industry in Canada," Norm says. "He really came through."

The employees pulled together too, despite their fears that Norm might just decide to close down. James remembers that fateful weekend. "Most people [staff] came to my apartment. Everyone wanted to know: 'What's Norm going to do–are we going to stay in business?' It would've been easy for him to call it quits; he was 58 or so, and it wasn't like he needed the cash. He was frustrated with 20 years of dealing with tough customers. And he got offers from the competition to buy out the Wallace name."

But in the end, the employees were relieved to learn that Norm wasn't interested in selling, or quitting. "He felt the 30 employees were more important than that–that was the bottom line," James says. "And

the purchase offers might've spurred him on; given him even *more* vigour to keep going. You know…to say, 'I'll show *you*.'"

Norm was deeply moved by all the support shown to him, and his family and the company after the fire, and it fueled a strong need to give back to the community which had been there for him and Agnes when they needed it most.

Empathy with aboriginals

Norm volunteered his time on the Family Service Bureau and SaskNative Economic Development Corporation (SNEDCO), and founded Saskatoon's first halfway house for convicted felons attempting to make a productive transition back into society, in 1976. Norm often visited the house to talk with the men. He was fascinated by their stories of how they'd ended up in trouble. Many of the men were aboriginal, and Norm related to their childhood difficulties growing up in homes where the addictions of parents cause the suffering of children and the cycle of abuse, and addiction, that can result. The men trusted

11

him because he wasn't a bureaucrat, and because he listened to them and actively found them work. Norm placed many of the residents in the construction industry as drywallers, and in the Mitchell's Gourmet Foods meatpacking plant. The model was so successful that the government of the day eventually bought a home and staffed it using the same principles.

His affinity for, and work with, aboriginal business leaders and chiefs continued as he looked for opportunities to open up offshore market opportunities for them. In one instance, in 1987, he paid for four Saskatchewan chiefs to conduct an economic trade mission to South Africa, where he knew there was great trade potential. The representatives were Lindsay Cyr (chief of Pasqua), Eldon Bellgarde (district chief of Ft. Qu'Appelle), Brian Tootoosis (councillor of Poundmaker) and Gerald Wuttanee (former chief of Red Pheasant).

This was one of the early opportunities for Saskatchewan's aboriginal people to begin looking outside their province and country for potential economic development. Gerald Wuttanee says the trip was a huge success.

"When we arrived in Pretoria, Glenn Babb [South African Ambassador to Canada] was there to meet us," Gerald says. "He hugged me, and said, 'Gerald, you wanna meet the press? It's just a scrum.' I said ok, and he took us into the big ballroom of a famous old hotel."

When the chiefs walked in, the imagined press audience of 10 or 20 people was actually a room packed full of reporters–2,000 of them. They were from all over the world, and included Time, Macleans, and the major Toronto newspapers. The chiefs ascended the platform, dazed from their long journey and the unexpected attention, and began answering questions.

"Joe Clark had landed in Johannesburg the same day," Gerald recalls. "They asked me what I thought of our foreign minister." At the time, the Canadian government was scolding South Africa for its apartheid policies. "I said, 'I think Joe Clark should clean up his own back yard before he goes to other countries,'" Gerald says. Asked to elaborate, Gerald and the other representatives began telling the press about the state of Canada's aboriginal population.

"Well, everyone covered it, it was news on every station, in every paper," Gerald says. "Pik Bhota [South Africa's foreign affairs minister] met Clark at the airport and apparently tore him apart, about natives dying young, etc. He got all that information from the press coverage."

The reporters were also waiting to ask the chiefs why there was so much opposition in Canada to them coming to South Africa. "The universities were knocking us down, because of associating with a racist government," Gerald says, "but we said, 'We want to go, it's our business. We want to show the world how the natives are being treated here.' The FSIN had been to China 10 years before us, and there was a little piece in the Star Phoenix right beside the obits. But us, we hit the world news."

So, in addition to starting to build trade bridges between the aboriginal business community and other countries, the trip Norm backed also had the effect of raising awareness and understanding of the plight of Canada's aboriginal people on a worldwide scale.

Soon after, Chief Louis Stevenson invited 300 reporters to the Peguis First Nation reserve outside Winnipeg to create awareness about the poor living conditions on Canadian reserves. "Yet another barrier started to fall," Norm says. "The reporters, who'd never been on a reserve, came away stunned at how bad things were, and how little they had realized it. This kind of education, along with starting to build relationships off the reserves and outside Canada, were great sources of empowerment."

Why do aboriginal people trust Norm? Simple, says Gerald. "Norm has dealt with the native people, and he deals good. No problems. He keeps his word…that's the main thing."

Stubbornness: weakness and strength

Being who he is, Norm has also acquired his share of detractors. "My wife says my biggest weakness is my stubbornness, but, luckily, she's learned to live with it." Others...not so much.

As one person said, "If Norm disagrees with something, he starts a splinter group." He's been described by opponents as a "pit bull," "aggravating as hell," and other even more colourful phrases one can't publish. He has no trouble calling a person an "idiot," a "Communist," or any other descriptive moniker that fits with his passion of the moment.

But he has a generous, kind and easy-going flip side that balances him, and inspires great loyalty from those with whom he works. So much so, that the highly-experienced senior staff will someday retire, and the company needs to make sure that new blood is coming in and learning from the elders. Dale, 55, says he could, but doesn't want to, retire. "I like

Norm, staff, customers and manufacturers celebrate Wallace Construction's 30th Anniversary in 2002.

coming to work so much, what would the point of retiring be?" James agrees. "The last couple of years I worked in construction, I hated to get up in the morning and go to work. But I enjoy coming here. It's a good place."

Long-time community colleague Kent Smith-Windsor, executive director of the Greater Saskatoon

A Wallace insulation project for Brunskill School in Saskatoon. Insulation is one of the 70 product lines in 36 categories that Wallace distributes.

Chamber of Commerce, sums it up: "The nature of Norm is that he's a fierce friend and a fierce foe–and which he is can depend on the issue. You're either with him or agin' him on every issue. There's no holds barred." As a friend, Smith-Windsor says, Norm is tough and rugged, but self-accountable and demanding of the same from others.

"His loyalty to Saskatoon or Canada can never be questioned," Kent says. "That's unwavering." Norm's dedication to his community may not be visible to everyone, but it is clearly borne out by the numerous projects he undertakes to help others. Kent says that most people don't realize the extent of Norm's softer side. "He keeps his own personal contributions to activities pretty quiet. He's been involved helping people in the health area, and has done work in First Nations communities." Norm has also helped numerous young entrepreneurs get support to start their businesses.

Former business columnist, Paul Martin, wrote of Norm at the time of the Wallace fire: "For all his noise, he has a streak of generosity that few in this province's business community can match. In particular, he has a soft spot for anyone trying to get ahead; for people willing to risk their own capital to build a business or trying to improve the community. He doesn't hesitate to put up his own money to lure a business to Saskatchewan or to back an upstart. And he does all of this quietly, without fanfare."[2]

Norm has gone to bat for people, even when it wasn't necessarily in his best interests. "Seven years ago, he was buddies with a guy in Alberta, a distributor like us, who won a competitive bid against us for a major roof membrane and insulation project," James recalls. "Something like $600,000 to $800,000 of business. Just after that, a federal anti-dumping law came through, and this specific insulation was included on the list. So it was going to be tough, and costly, for this guy to get his material across the border.

"He called Norm and asked for help. I said, 'Norm, he just took $500,000 out of your pocket–how can you help him?' Norm looked surprised; he hadn't even thought of it that way. He was the only private businessman in the country who went to the tribunal to argue against this law, and it was to help this guy."

Persistence and the ability to look to the future are essential qualities of successful entrepreneurship, Kent says. "No entrepreneur can be successful without a 'never give up' attitude. Norm is very change-friendly and it has helped his business become quite successful. He's always been comfortable with letting go of what has been, and looking at what could be. You need people like Norm who are willing to press for change to keep a community on its game," he continues. "A community should always be a wee bit uncomfortable in its own skin."

If you ask Norm what his greatest strength is, there's no hesitation in his response. "Definitely the support of my wife, Agnes," he says. "It's lonely being on your own. The initial years of being in your own business are very lean. You have to have a partner who is okay with that wild kind of life."

His sons are both doing well in their professions (one will likely take over operation of Wallace Construction) and, for the first time, Norm's becoming quite hopeful about the changes he sees happening in the province's prosperity. "I think we're heading in the right direction, finally," he says. "We have a dynamic community, a small Calgary. Not that long ago, other countries didn't want to do business with us, because government policies and other nonsense made it so difficult. China used to hate us, but today we're involved with them in food processing. Business is getting done. That's what we've needed for decades, to provide jobs–that's what builds prosperity for everyone, not just the rich."

But then, Norm has known that all along. As Martin noted in his column, Norm was keen to reinvest in Saskatoon after his losses in the fire, rather than move. As far back as 1996, Norm was proudly declaring, "There are more opportunities in Saskatoon today than anywhere else in Canada."[4]

So, what's next for Norm?

He'll continue to support the work of the Prairie Policy Centre, which he helped found in 2001. The institute is self-described as an "…independent, non-partisan, not-for-profit research and educational organization that advances ideas on wealth creation in order to enhance the economic and social well-being of Saskatchewan, the Prairie Region, and Canada as a whole."[3]

He'll continue to focus energy on the newest crop of Saskatchewan entrepreneurs. From 1968 to 1976, the University of Saskatchewan's College of Commerce held an entrepreneurial competition similar to the current Canadian television show "Dragon's Den" in which people (in this case, commerce students) with business ideas made pitches to a panel of venture capitalists. Norm was one of those "dragons," and invested, on average, in one budding entrepreneur per year through that program alone.

James says, "Norm wants to help the local economy…he's never forgotten that he started with nothing."

"I hope to continue starting many new businesses with young entrepreneurs, and I'd like to help people market patents," Norm says. "I've always loved seeing young people I've worked with make successes of their companies and have their children grow up to follow in their footsteps. It's very rewarding."

It's a legacy of creating something from nothing that sits very well with the brash kid from Dublin.

Workers lay Styrofoam "void forms" for the Mother Theresa School project in Saskatoon. Similar to a cardboard version developed by Wallace, the forms create "breathing space" between shifting ground and cement floors, reducing the potential for cracks.

Herb Pinder
Play hard, work harder

It was that magical week between Christmas and New Year's…when people take a break from their lives to hunker down, feast, rest and visit family. In 1967, that week in Winnipeg was also about hockey–the Centennial Tournament, to be exact. It was -40° C, but nobody cared–least of all the Pinder family.

Herb Sr. and his wife, Shirley, from Saskatoon, had checked into the Hotel Fort Garry. The next night their two sons, Herb Jr. and Gerry, would be teaming up on the Canadian Nationals hockey team, the Nats, to face off against the formidable Russian team who, at that time, had rarely been beaten.

The night before the big game, Herb Sr. was planning how he could cram in a full day of work in Toronto, and still make it back in time to catch the game. "I can fly there in the morning, work all day, and be back by the time the puck drops," Herb Sr. assured his wife.

The next morning, he flew to Toronto, worked all day, and then accepted a ride to the airport from long-time friend, Willard "Bud" Estey (destined to become a Justice of the Supreme Court of Canada). All was going fine–until he arrived at the terminal.

"In those days there was no security," Herb says now. "You only had to arrive at the gate five minutes before the flight." Or so he thought. When he arrived, the plane was already backing away. Herb was dumbfounded. The game in Winnipeg was important, in itself, but it was also a prelude to the upcoming Winter Olympics in France where his sons would again be representing Canada. He had to get on that plane and make it back to Winnipeg.

He protested to the attendant, who agreed that the plane shouldn't leave early, but she was helpless to stop it. The airport manager was called in, but could only repeat that it was policy; there was nothing they could do–even though the flight was, indeed, taking off early.

"I was steaming at that point," Herb says, using polite language to describe what was surely a much stronger emotion.

Though he's a long-time member of Riverside Country Club, Herb Pinder Sr. started his golf career caddying at the Saskatoon Golf & Country Club (shown here) in the '30s. He's always tried to keep a healthy balance between entrepreneurial pursuits and family.

Herb Sr. shot this photo just minutes after his boys, Herb Jr. and Gerry, received their bronze medals at the '68 Grenoble Olympics.

"I just need to get there"

In desperation, Herb pleaded with the manager. "My boys are playing for Canada tonight against Russia in Winnipeg, and I have to be there!" The manager's eyes widened and, like any true Canadian hockey fan would, he immediately went into problem-solving mode. After making a few inquiries, he returned to the agitated father. Out of breath, he said, "Okay, would you be willing to go on a cargo flight?"

"I don't care how," Herb Sr. said, "I just need to get there!"

The manager got him into a vehicle that sped across the tarmac to a DC-8 just preparing for take off. The captain put a camp chair in the cargo hold and strapped a belt across Herb's lap. He sat there, freezing but determined, amongst the load of freight. He could've cared less about the temperature.

The Russians went on to win the game, but Herb Pinder had made it. He had seen his boys play.

Less than two months later, the Canadian team took the bronze medal in hockey at the 1968 Grenoble Winter Games, with each Pinder son adding a goal to the effort.

Herb Pinder is an "executive father"–a persistent and goal-oriented family man. He brings those qualities to his many entrepreneurial ventures, which included the highly successful Pinder Drug Store chain started by his father, Robert.

If there were genes for athletics and business, Herb Pinder inherited them from both sides of his family. The family of Herb's mother, Helen Rose, emigrated from Aberdeen, Scotland, landing in Antigonish in 1832. They moved west and have a large farming operation in Manitoba to this day.

Herb's paternal grandfather, Abram Pinder, immigrated to Canada from Yorkshire, England, around 1850; and started his own business, north of Toronto, as a lath and plaster contractor. Traveling by horse and buggy, he moved to wherever the job site was, following the work to Saskatoon in 1911.

Abram did the plaster work for the Saskatoon Sanatorium and St. Paul's Hospital. In the 1920s, Pinder Construction built 400 homes in Saskatoon. Then the Dirty Thirties arrived, and there wasn't a new house built for eight years in the city. Abram died in 1934 at 80, leaving a family that included Robert Mitford Pinder, Herb's father.

Robert apprenticed at Coad's Drug Store, now immortalized in Saskatoon's Western Development Museum "Boomtown" exhibit. He also became part of the local Pacific Coast Hockey League team, the Saskatoon Sheiks, (later renamed the Crescents) where he was a defenseman.

Robert dropped everything in 1912 to do a one-year program at the College of Pharmacy in Winnipeg (though he hadn't finished high school). Over time, he worked his way up to a partnership in the Saskatoon Drug and Stationery Company. In 1915, he purchased it outright. With credit from the bank, he created the first Pinders Drug Store.

Robert married Helen Rose in 1916, and they started a family soon after. Herb was the youngest (1923), after siblings Ross, Phyllis and Muriel.

In 1919, Robert purchased his old hockey team, the Saskatoon Crescents, which he owned for four or five years. Among his players were five members now in the Hockey Hall of Fame–Aurele Joliat, Bill Cook, George Hainsworth, Edouard "Newsy" Lalonde and Frank Frederickson.[1] "Huge names in hockey history," Herb says. "And he built a *business* during all of this."

By the 1920s, Robert had developed a major pharmacy business in Saskatoon and was expanding; building stores in North Battleford and Yorkton. Everyone did well in the boom times of the early 1920s, but when the Depression suffocated the North American economy, things got tough. Businesses all around Robert went bankrupt. "It was hand to mouth in the '30s," Herb says. "So many of Dad's friends went under. I guess it was because they had all learned to spend in the '20s, when there was a lot of money, and then had trouble cutting back soon enough." Robert Pinder survived, presumably because he didn't suffer from the same economic disorder as his friends.

In both business and athletic activities, Herb learned by example from his father. Robert Pinder was "hugely" active–not only as an entrepreneur but in public life, as well. He was a Saskatoon alderman from 1928-1933 and mayor from 1935-1938.[2] "He was busy, busy, busy–nothing was too much trouble to tackle," Herb says.

But Robert wasn't much for publicity. Herb recalls getting this advice from his dad when he was young: "Herb, there are two kinds of people–those who get things done, and the others who like to take credit for it. I recommend you be in the first group. There's a lot less competition." Modest by nature, Herb found this advice agreeable, and has lived his life as quietly as possible for a man with his large-scale achievements.

Sports, music and dancing

Herb says that kids "made their own fun" in the '30s, and worked if they could. He found the best of both worlds as a golf caddy at the Saskatoon Golf and Country Club (SGCC). "In those days there were no carts," he says. "Golfers took caddies on every round. There were a lot of caddies. SGCC and Riverside were Saskatoon's only courses."

After his first year at the University of Saskatchewan, the 17-year-old hitchhiked to Banff to spend the summer working as a caddy at the prestigious Banff Springs Golf Club. "Nobody got very much in those days," he says, "so I worked my way up to lifeguard, then into the hotel–running the elevators, and being a bellhop."

During that time, the Banff Springs Hotel was the summer location for one of Canada's most popular radio shows, hosted by the Big Band conductor Mart Kenney and his band, The Western Gentlemen. He entertained hotel guests and broadcast live from the hotel's Alhambra Room on CBC. Having played saxophone in the Saskatoon Boys Band, the young Herb loved to hang around the band, sitting in the odd time at band rehearsals and dancing

Robert Pinder, invited as a Saskatchewan MLA (member of the legislature), awaits a handshake from King George VI on his royal visit to Canada in 1939, which included a stop in Saskatoon on June 4.

at the parties the band held for the hotel staff after guests had retired for the evening. He eventually got to know Mart quite well.

Returning to school in the fall each year, Herb studied and played hard. He lettered in football, basketball and swimming, but his great love was golf. Herb would be a competitive amateur well into his senior years, playing with Canadian greats—like the legendary Moe Norman. In 1979, he joined the Canadian Senior Golf Association and played a number of times on the national team that competed bi-annually with teams from the United Kingdom and the United States.

Golf was more than a sport to Herb in his younger years; it also helped him get through one of the most difficult periods of his life.

Golf: an oasis from war

After graduating from university and Navy reserve training, Herb moved to Halifax in the summer of 1942 to attend the four-month officer's training program at King's College. After graduation, he was supposed to get two weeks leave before being assigned overseas to the Royal Navy. He had arranged to spend his leave visiting girlfriend Shirley Hughes in London, Ontario, and then slipping out to Saskatoon to see his parents. It was his last chance for a proper goodbye before going off to war. Herb, naturally, had his golf clubs in tow—so he could play during his off hours from training. His plan was to take them back home on his leave. However, a call the night before graduation changed all those plans. A British cruiser had come into Halifax Harbour.

"My commanding officer called and said, 'We're boarding tonight and we sail in the morning,'" Herb

Herb on his ship, the HMS Keppel, in the Thames Estuary, with brother, Ross, visiting from the Army in 1943.

recalls. "I had to phone Shirley and my dad. If you said, 'I'm in Halifax and I'm sailing tomorrow,' the phone call would be cut off. All I could say was, 'I'll be back in two years.' Dad said, 'They can't do that.' I said, 'Yah, Dad, they can.'"

The 19-year-old grabbed his golf clubs (he had nowhere to leave them) and his gear, and reported for duty. Along with three other young men from his class, he was posted to a Royal Navy destroyer and spent two years at sea, traveling from the Mediterranean to South Africa to Northern Russia, and seeing "considerable action"–mostly anti-submarine and anti-aircraft warfare.

Though "action" was what most 19-year-old soldiers were looking for, they didn't realize how horrifying it would actually be. During that time, Herb was able to offset some of that terrible duty by playing golf when the destroyer pulled into port to refuel and refresh supplies. Since he had his clubs with him, his commanding officer would invite Herb ashore to play a round. As a result, the young golfer lived a dream that many golfers have, but few realize. He played all the great Scottish links courses, including the most famous

of all–the Old Course at St. Andrews, generally recognized as the birthplace of golf. Golf rounds became an oasis of normalcy in the midst of conflict; and the focus required to play a round turned out to be a great distraction from the stresses of war.

In 1944, after participating in the invasion of Normandy, Herb returned to Canada and the Canadian Navy as a "more or less" seasoned executive officer of a Navy frigate, and he and Shirley got engaged. He was recalled from leave in September 1944. For another a year and a half he served as First Lieutenant (second in command) of the frigate HMCS Prestonian, and then the destroyer HMCS Qu'Appelle. He was discharged in December 1945.

During his war career, Herb's ship sank three German U-boats in the North Atlantic and the Arctic Circle. They were events and years that left an indelible mark on him.

Looking for a purpose

When he was discharged from the Navy, Herb wasn't sure what to do next. "I assumed Ross would come back [from the Army] and partner with my dad, so I couldn't see any future for me in the family business," Herb says.

Shirley's brother had been killed in action while Herb was away. Her father had also died. She had no other family in London, Ontario. "She had a very unhappy time then," Herb says. "You know, 4,000 Saskatchewan people were killed in that war, and our population was less than a million. When the war came along, people flocked to the military because, at the time, there were no jobs."

Herb and Shirley graduate from the same class at the University of Saskatchewan in 1942.

At one point during the war, on leave from the ship in the Boston Navy Yard, Herb had taken a trip to Cambridge, wandering around the Harvard University campus where he became "quite interested" in the business school. He interviewed with the assistant dean and put in a post-war application. There were 3,000 applications overall. Herb was among 20 Canadians who entered Harvard's first post-war MBA class, in February 1946.

Herb and Shirley married in January 1946, and immediately headed to Harvard so he could begin his studies. "Our honeymoon was a train ride to Cambridge," he says.

That same year, the unthinkable happened. Robert Pinder died suddenly of a stroke, at the young age of 55. Herb and his family were stunned and heart-broken. "He [my father] was almost larger than life because he was so involved and busy and strong," says Herb. "To have him felled with no warning was such a shock. He just went to bed one night and didn't wake up."

Herb came home for the funeral, and then returned to Cambridge where he finished his MBA, graduating in 1947.

Pinder's trucks outside the first store on 21st and 2nd Avenue, Saskatoon, in the 1950s.

With his brother, Ross, just out of the services, Herb and Shirley decided to come back to Saskatoon (after his graduation) so Herb could help out with the Saskatoon Drug & Stationery Company. Their young family was growing and Shirley decided that Saskatoon was where she wanted to raise the kids. Their first son, Herb Jr., had been born during their first year in Boston, and two more sons, Gerry and Richard, were born in the two years following their return home.

"If you really want to stay here," Herb told Shirley, "I'm going to have to be away a lot." Shirley agreed to look after the kids, which now included two more children, Tom and Patty–bringing the newest generation of Pinders to a total of five.

The lifetime partnership of Herb and Shirley was critical to his ability to successfully build a business. "I can't underestimate what Shirley's support meant," Herb says "In terms of her nurturing of the children, and allowing me to do what I had to do. It was the only way we could be successful in both business and in raising the family, *both* of which were important."

"Ross was president of Pinders Drugs, and I joined him on the financial and real estate end of the business," Herb says of joining the company in 1947.

Oil and land

That year, the great Leduc light crude oil discovery in Alberta made big headlines. Leduc was the largest discovery in Canada in 33 years, and triggered a boom that would lead to the discovery of the bulk of Canada's oil reserves, hidden deep in the limestone and dolomite reefs of Devonian Era rock.[3]

At the time, all the American companies had Canadian headquarters in Regina, not in Alberta. "At that time, Saskatoon and Regina weren't very big," Herb says. "If something was going on, it wasn't hard to know about it. We found there were dozens of American lease hounds leasing mineral rights in Saskatchewan. You couldn't be in Saskatoon long before you'd run into someone with an American accent."

Excited by the investment opportunity, Herb joined a group of six long-time friends to see if they could raise enough capital to get in on the action. "We knew that the oil discovery was significant, but we didn't know anything about the oil business," Herb says. They were like Panasonic, Herb says, "A few years ahead of our time." That vision, and willingness to take a risk, would change their lives.

In 1949, the group decided to start a drilling company with $25,000 raised between them.

They made a deal to buy a drilling rig for $250,000, and the supply company agreed to sell the rig for 10% down–coincidentally, the exact amount the group had raised. They were in the oil business.

Forming a private oil company, Devonian Petroleums Ltd., they sold shares to friends to raise capital. They started leasing land from farmers for drilling in southeast Saskatchewan, and were one of the companies to receive a large "drilling reservation" of 100,000 acres from the Saskatchewan government. A drilling reservation was a chunk of land owned by the government to which a company would receive primary drilling and exploration rights, with return obligations to the government.

In 1952, their efforts paid off, as they struck oil–the first light crude oil discovery in Saskatchewan. "It was huge," Herb says. "It's now in the Steelman Field, with several hundred wells."

The oil company went public under the name Canadian Devonian Petroleums (CDP), and was listed on the Toronto and New York Stock Exchanges after a deal with Gulf Oil. New and significant discoveries were made by CDP, but they were out of the business by 1962–due to what Herb calls an "unfriendly" takeover. Their success was undeniable: Shareholders did well in the buy-out and, at the end, CDP held half-interest in 225 oil wells in southeast Saskatchewan, Alberta and the U.S.

To accommodate the real estate needs of growing and diverse business interests, the Pinder brothers created the Saskatoon Trading Company Ltd., which became the property management company for the drug stores and all other ventures. It was a good move.

With it, they could purchase the land on which drugstores sat. They no longer had to worry about unpredictable and costly increases in land leases, giving them much greater stability.

The '60s also brought political wrangles between business and both the provincial and federal governments over the succession duty. When an owner died, and a business was passed down in the family, they had to pay a duty to the governments of 50% of the current value of the company. "Succession duties became much more important to the entrepreneurial community than to big industry," Herb says. "In public companies, you could just sell more shares. But if you were private, what did you do–sell half the factory?" In some cases, this is exactly what happened. Smaller companies were often forced to close stores, lay off workers or, at the worst, go out of business entirely in order to pay the tax. With each passing generation, companies got smaller and smaller, until they just disappeared.

This policy got Herb Pinder's dander up. "Bowman Brothers, in Saskatoon, was the largest privately owned auto parts distributorship in North America," he says of one sad example. "They had distributorships from Toronto to Vancouver, and were people I knew well. When a partner died, the succession duty forced them to contract considerably, until they just went the way of all flesh. It was a crying shame. The taxes the government collected didn't come *close* to making up for what was lost in entrepreneurship of that company–its value to the community in jobs and so many other areas."

In 1977, the provincial government ended the duty, replacing it with the current capital gains tax.[4] The end result, however, was that many entrepreneurs

In the 1950s, merchandise was still behind counters. A cosmetic company rep completes a purchase with Pinders President Ross Pinder, brother of Herb.

moved out of province and the benefits of their success were lost to Saskatchewan. "It's one of the reasons there are so few fourth-generation family-owned businesses in this province," Herb says.

Shopping malls and ranches

Herb's son, Tom, has vivid memories of his father's entrepreneurial spirit. "As a child, I remember my father was always very busy and into a new venture of some sort, business or otherwise. If he saw something in his travels and thought it was appropriate for Saskatoon–he would just make it happen."

A perfect example was the idea of bringing the shopping mall to Saskatchewan. In the early '50s, Herb saw the brand-new North Hill shopping centre in Calgary, the first in Western Canada. The concept of the shopping mall so impressed him that he returned to Saskatoon fired up to make the same thing happen in his province. In 1956, the Pinders' Saskatoon Trading Company was instrumental, along with developer Cliff McClocklin in building Saskatchewan's first shopping mall–the Churchill Shopping Centre. The team made a proposal to double the two-acre size originally offered by the city, but the planning department wouldn't go for it. "The city planners at that time didn't have a lot of experience with this kind of thing," Herb says, "and they said it would be plenty big for that neighbourhood. Well, it became hugely successful and wasn't expandable."

That experience was an important business lesson. "It taught me something about getting into ventures that weren't expandable. All my life since then, I've tried not to get into ventures that don't have expansion possibilities."

In the late '50s, a project with all kinds of expansion opportunities presented itself.

John Minor was a third-generation dry land rancher in his 30s who, with his wife Gertie and a family of young cowboys, operated Saskatchewan's largest private ranch. Minor Ranch at Abbey was near the Great Sand Hills in the southwest corner of the province, and contained 90 sections (59,000 acres) of dry land farming and ranching.

Herb had befriended John, admiring his pluck for eking out a sizable ranch under difficult terrain conditions. "He was a bright and very hard-working operator with great vision and ambition to do big things," Herb says, including conducting the first on-range artificial insemination program with a better than 95% calf crop.

The huge and famous Chilco Ranch in British Columbia had become available for sale. Believing he could grow the ranch to 9,000 head of cattle, John collected a large group of investors to raise the capital to purchase it. One of those investors was Herb.

The Chilco Ranch sat between the Rockies and the Coastal Range, and west of Williams Lake. A vast one million acres, much of it on grazing leases from the Department of Forestry at the junction of the Chilcotin and Fraser rivers, Herb says it was mountain ranching reminiscent of the *Bonanza* of television fame. "It was full of timber, streams, creeks and lakes, with wildlife galore."

Unfortunately, tragedy struck in 1962. The cook's grandson became desperately ill and John offered to fly them into Vancouver in his Piper. Weather caused a crash, and all three were killed. With his passing, came the death of the vision for

Chilco Ranch. Not being able to replace John's passion, determination and experience for the project, the group had to sell the ranch. "It was the end of John's life and dream," Herb says. "It was also the end of one of the most imaginative projects in which I was ever involved."

A political interlude

Like his father, Herb dabbled in politics, but soon learned it wasn't the life for him.

He got involved in the Tommy Douglas era of Saskatchewan politics in the 1960s, when the only opposition was the Liberal Party–at the time, the party of free enterprise and free trade. He eventually became party president, and a cabinet minister in Ross Thatcher's government. "Those are things dear to my heart," Herb says. "I learned from my grand-father that free enterprise was private enterprise, and free trade was the basis of all Western Canada. Without free trade, we wouldn't be able to do much."

As minister of industry and commerce, in charge of the Crown power corporation (SaskPower), in 1964, Herb's long-held beliefs of not getting involved with business you don't understand came to the forefront. "Politicians spend more time trying to run companies they don't know anything about…I was chairman of the board of the power corporation… What did I know about running such a business? That made no sense to me. My experience was that a board chair of a corporation needs a deep background and clear understanding of the business.

"Then we'd change governments, and new people would suddenly be running those huge corporations. They were all nice fellas, don't get me

"We dressed this way every day back then," says Herb of these natty three-piece suits sported by him (right) and Ross in the 1950s on 2nd Avenue in Saskatoon.

wrong, but they don't know *anything* about the businesses of insurance, phones, power, gas or pipelining." This major chasm between his business experience and political reality created a disconnect of values he couldn't live with and, in 1965, he officially retired from politics.

Herb's powerful memory is a part of his character and personality "that people seem to adore," says son Dick. "Apart from being well educated and very well read, Dad has an amazing power of recall. This talent sets him apart and engages endless numbers of people in his experiences and recollections of people, places and other details otherwise lost."

Herb is also skilled in the nearly-lost art of conversation, Dick says. "He loves, and has a great ability, to debate. Any sort of discussion, whether business or social. He's famous for debating people at parties in fairly elaborate discussion, and he draws heavily on common sense, vast knowledge, and insatiable curiosity. He satisfies that curiosity through engaging with people, and voracious reading."

Herb Jr. recalls an incident illustrating Herb's great resourcefulness and ability to think on his feet. "Dad's a rugged individualist, he doesn't go with the flow," he says. "He thinks things through independently, and of course, he hates paying unnecessary taxes. I once went to Whitefish, Montana, and bought a new pair of skis. At the border, we were told the value of skis was above my personal exemption limit. So Dad says, on the spot, 'We'll each declare one ski.' Well, they couldn't argue with that."

Herb had good mentors, and became one himself, especially to his children. Former Chicago Blackhawks player Gerry Pinder says his dad taught all of them, mostly by example, how to behave in life and business. Herb did Gerry a favour[5] when he first went into pro hockey. In return, he asked his son to promise that when he finished his hockey career he would go back to university and finish his business degree. Nine years later, due to eye injuries, Gerry's career ended much sooner than he'd imagined. His father immediately asked him if he remembered his promise. "I didn't, but as soon as he reminded me, I knew I had to go back and finish. There was no option. And I'm very grateful for that lesson of always doing what you promise, no matter what, and also the value he placed on education. It gave me, at 30, a much better start in life than I would've otherwise had."

Taking pride in industry innovation

As far back as the 1950s, the Pinders readily implemented new ideas when they made good business sense. Herb looks back on the innovations and strengths of the Pinder organization–like being the first drugstore in Western Canada to operate with open shelving. "When I first started, everything was behind a counter," Herb says. "Customers couldn't get to the merchandise; they had to be served. It sounds ludicrous now, but that's the way it was."

A decade later, they would introduce the idea of the convenience store in Saskatoon, eventually opening three such locations starting in 1964–five years prior to the introduction of the first 7-Eleven in Canada.[6]

Because it was not a core business, it was bypassed for its strategic potential, however, it planted the seed for another innovation in the 1970s–the notion of putting convenience food in expanded drugstores, which, again, Pinders was the first to do in the Canadian drug store industry.

In-mall stores followed free-standing stores.
This is the Pinders at Midtown Plaza, Saskatoon, in 1991.

Then came the revolution in store hours in the 1970s. "Drug stores used to operate like banks," Herb says. "They had short hours. Our operators suggested we start keeping stores in Saskatoon and Regina open until midnight. Our competitors, who thought they had to emulate us, were upset with us for disturbing the quiet ways of drug stores."

Later, under Dick's leadership, came another Canadian innovation–'point of sale' systems. "Before, all merchandise was hand-marked or stickered," Herb says. New computer-based tracking systems created efficiencies and accuracies from the point of sale at the register, all the way back to tracking inventory and accounting for it.

End of an era

In 1993, the Pinders sold most of their family retail business to Shoppers Drug Mart, ending more than 75 years in the pharmacy business. At its peak, Pinders Drugs included 21 locations with 500 employees. It had been quite an achievement.

But before that, Herb's two sons–Herb Jr. and then, Dick–ran Pinders for a total of nearly two decades. Gerry and Tom were directors, and Patty was co-owner of the holding company. "The business got well into the third generation," Dick says. The decision to sell was "emotional," and a tough one, but "…it was the right thing to do, and the right time to do it," Dick says.

The Pinders sold the distribution business, a year later, and the Pinder name, having been lit up on the signs of many community pharmacies for three generations, was replaced by the now-familiar Shoppers Drug Mart logo.

A family photo montage from the 1960s. Clockwise from top left is Dick, Shirley, Herb Sr., Herb Jr., Gerry, Patty and Tom.

Since a heart attack and surgery in 1982, and the loss of his beloved wife Shirley in 2007, Herb has lessened his traveling but, at 86, is still plenty active in business. When asked what he thinks his father's greatest achievement is, son Dick says, "Notwithstanding Dad's great accomplishments from childhood (completing three grades in one year); exemplary service in World War II, and many more high pursuits in business, politics, golf … his 'finest hour' was his devotion and return of dedication to my mother during her years as a victim of Alzheimer's disease. He was determined to keep her in their home through the late stages of her suffering and he succeeded, at some considerable risk to his own health."

The five Pinder children have all become successful in their own rights, and Herb sees that as a logical extension of the legacy of his grandfather, his father and himself–passing down the work ethic that he learned as a kid shagging balls on the range and shouldering the golf bags of club members.

The Early & Bloski Families

Seeds of risk

June 22, 1993

Dear Tom,

It's a small world! I'm in Winnipeg for a weekend, and I meet one of your buddies! You can imagine how happy I was to hear through him that you are in good health…

I could not help but fill him in on the enormous help I got from your father (Spencer A.) and you when I started out in Canada 38 years ago. Matter of fact, in 1956, you shipped rapeseed on an open account valued at a few hundred thousand dollars, which I sold for you in Europe and paid for after my customers remitted. I was 23 years old then, and did not have a penny in assets. Now, 38 years later, I want to again thank you and your late father for the confidence you placed in me at that crucial time of my new career in Canada…

…One more thing: In the meantime, you have become a good customer of ours and it is about time that I confirm to you your line of open credit with us: Tom, this line of open credit is set at $1 million and if this is not sufficient, please contact me and I will make a further adjustment.

Keep well and stay healthy.

With fondest regards, Rolf C. Hagen[1]

Spencer Early and Joe Bloski in front of an original seed cabinet from the 1920s, which is still used today.

The earliest Early

The recipient of this momentous letter was Tom Early, son of Spencer Abner (S.A.) Early. In 1907, S.A. founded a hay, grain and feed store in a small frame building in Saskatoon that, over its first century, was to become a major Western Canadian retailer of feed, seed, pet and garden products with annual sales around $10 million.

The letter tells an amazing story of the trust, risk-taking and character judgment that so defined the entrepreneur S.A. Early. What had he known about the young upstart from Germany, who barely had enough change to buy him lunch when they met in July 1956 at the Eiffel Tower restaurant, on Stanley Street, in Montreal? Did he know that after barely being able to pay the bill and sighing with relief, the young entrepreneur went pale when S.A. ordered a brandy with his coffee?

"There went the tip for the waiter," Hagen recalled in the same letter. "I think I was even a few cents short on the total bill. I just stole away, but the drink may have tipped the scales, because obviously I got a good credit rating from your dad."[2]

Did the wise assessor of character recognize, in this young German, a solid man of integrity; who he knew wouldn't take his valuable product across the ocean and never be seen again? Did he somehow intuit that this man would build a $700 million a year empire in pet products, and repay S.A.'s initial trust in him many times over? Or, did he just want to help out a young entrepreneur? To S.A., the latter would have been well worth the risk.

The sentiments expressed by Hagen, nearly four decades after this memorable meeting, are an impressive illustration of the role that trust and relationship development plays in the building of a business. No one understood that better than S.A. Early.

Blended family business

The Early's company story was built on the hard work and keen judgment of two generations of Earlys, and then continued by the addition of two men from a different family—Joe and John Bloski. Eventually, other family members from both clans (including Spencer, grandson of the founder; and Joe's two sons, Derek and Kevin) joined Early's, and today's company is a strong and successful blend of these two families.

The Early's history goes back to the family's move from Ireland to Canada in the 1840s. They settled in Ontario and, in 1905, two cousins traveled to homestead in Elstow. After some experience working at a custom threshing operation out of Elstow, S.A. and J. Hunter Early moved into Saskatoon to start their own businesses. S.A. started his hay, grain and feed store and J. Hunter began a fruit and produce sales operation.

In addition to his own business, S.A. worked with his cousin until J. Hunter left to start a Dodge-Chrysler

The original store on Wall Street opened in 1910.

The Earlys location on Idylwyld from 1917 to 1983.

car dealership, which is still in existence. S.A. carried on with his hay, grain and feed business on Wall Street. In 1914, he purchased a half-acre of land on Idylwyld Drive, and built a new grain elevator and a feed store, which opened in 1917, and stood as Saskatoon landmarks until 1983 when they were torn down. Though the country was in the midst of the Great Depression, S.A.'s venture grew. He built a second elevator in 1928, which allowed him to expand into the livestock feed manufacturing and seed grain cleaning business, and then into the garden seed packet trade. In 1942, S.A. Early & Co. published its first spring catalogue, which contained products for sale such as grains, grasses, feeds, poultry and livestock supplies, vegetable and flower seeds, pet food and supplies, and something new…baby-chicks–a product of Early's own hatchery.[2]

"My grandfather was the kind of entrepreneur, and I've met others like him since, who had to have a lot of things going on all the time," says Spencer Early, the current president of the company. "He built the elevator at Aylsham; he had a hog farm, the hatchery, the feed companies. Not all of it was financially successful, but that's what entrepreneurs do–they have all these ideas and they have to pursue them; they're just wired that way. They don't just sit on their laurels, they start something and they're on to the next project. He was the perfect example of that."

S.A. Early: larger than life

S.A. was a flamboyant and colourful man. In addition to multiple business interests and a large family raised by him and wife, Letitia, in their home on Poplar Crescent, S.A. was also active in the community.

He was a founder of the Nutana Curling Club, a city alderman for 14 years, and a member of the Saskatoon Collegiate Board. "The early riverbank development was a result of the foresight of men like my grandfather," Spencer says. At the turn of the century, these visionary men recognized the South Saskatchewan River as an enormous asset, and they prepared the way for today's development by establishing the parks along the riverbank. The riverbank is now central to Saskatoon's downtown culture and tourism–boasting over 300 acres of riverbank, parks and trails, as well as serving as the perfect setting for numerous festivals, the Mendel Art Gallery and Persephone Theatre.

Driving a big DeSoto automobile, sporting a jaunty fedora and smoking a cigar, S.A. was a familiar figure in Saskatoon, and everyone who knew him has a story. Spencer says, "One day, the well-known sports caster Lloyd Saunders says to me, 'I worked for your grandfather in the summer of '49, when I was

The Early grain elevator at Aylsham.

in high school. He used to give me the keys to his DeSoto to go buy cigars for him.'"

A lifetime member of the Riverside Country Club, S.A. helped out car-less caddies by picking them up and driving them out to their jobs at the club. Long-time Saskatoon Golf & Country Club head professional, Bill Turnbull, told Spencer, "I was a caddy as a kid. We'd wait on the corner of Lorne and Ruth Streets to be picked up. Your grandfather wouldn't let us sit on the seats of the DeSoto, because we were dusty. We had to sit on the floor."

In 1937, tragedy struck the Early family. S.A.'s 18-year-old son, Allan, who had already begun working for his father, was accidentally shot by his best friend while hunting, and died of his injuries.

Allan's younger brother, Tom, who'd just finished grade 12 the year before, hadn't planned to go into the family business. "My uncle, Allan, was the one who was interested in the business," Spencer says. "My dad told me that if Allan hadn't died, he [Tom] might never have become involved." But, given the circumstances, S.A. asked Tom to join him at Early's. Though

he hadn't planned to become an Early employee, once on board, Tom committed himself to the company with a dedication that rivaled his father's.

The business changed names in 1948, from S.A. Early & Company to Early Seed & Feed Ltd., to better reflect its changing product lines. S.A. was president, and Tom became general manager. The company flourished under the father-son management team through the 1950s.

In 1962, S.A. died, leaving his entrepreneurial legacy to his son, Tom, and four other children (not active in the company). The Earlys would soon be joined by another family who would help create a new era of growth through hard work, risk and reward.

You bet!

In 1966, Tom Early was struggling to find a good manager. He settled on 30-year-old seed company sales representative Joe Bloski to manage the seed division. "This was significant," says Spencer, "because Joe's still here. If it wasn't for that event, who knows whether the Early's Company would've kept going or not?"

"I'd been working for a competitor of sorts; a small company," Joe remembers. "There was a big fire in 1955, and the business was wiped out. I went to Speers Seed Store Limited and worked there for nine years. It was also a small business, and I wanted the opportunity to move on–which I got when I was hired as a salesman by seed giant A.E. McKenzie in 1964." McKenzie moved Joe and his family to Brandon.

Ironically, Saskatchewan was part of Joe's new territory. "One of my clients was Early's. I had met the president, Tom Early, when I was at Speers, and we had a good relationship. So, my first call was on him.

When I dropped in, we went to his office and he said, 'Jeez, why didn't you tell me you were looking to make a change? I'd have given you a job right off the bat.' Well, we hit it off right there and then. He invited me for dinner that night and I said, 'I'll see how things go in Brandon.'"

A year later, McKenzie wanted to transfer Joe and his family again, this time to Toronto. With his wife's family back in Saskatoon, and two young boys to raise, the big city "…started to look like another part of the world," according to Joe. Remembering Mr. Early's offer of the previous year, Joe dropped a note to him. As soon as he received it, Tom Early phoned Joe. "I'd asked him in the note if he remembered the conversation and if the offer to join Early's was still open. When I picked up the phone, it was Tom, and he said, 'You bet!'"

Tests of trust

Joe moved his family back to Saskatoon, and started working at Early's on August 1, 1966. He began working with seeds, an area with which he was very familiar. Unbeknown to him, however, he was actually being groomed to become a manager. Part of this grooming involved tests of trust by the boss.

"The first morning I came to work, we met at the door," Joe recalls. "He [Tom] reached into his pocket and handed me the key. He said he had to go pick up the mail, and that I should open up. I made sure I was there at that same time every morning. I joke with the guys that I've been opening up ever since."

Through these tests, Tom Early taught Joe the importance of building relationships of mutual trust and loyalty with employees. "Before the end of my

S.A. Early with son Tom, who had just joined the family business in the late '30s.

first year with him, with no accrued holiday time, he asked me to attend a convention in Edmonton because he couldn't go," Joe says. The convention was a big deal. Tom suggested to Joe that he might as well take his wife and make it a holiday, "while you're at it."

Surprised, Joe asked him how much time he should take. Tom said, "Take as much as you need to do it up right." Joe couldn't believe it, but he knew enough not to disappoint his boss by taking undue advantage.

"He showed me trust, but I'll tell you, if I'd abused that opportunity and fairness in him, and stayed away six weeks, he would have learned something about my trustworthiness and loyalty. Of course, I didn't stay away long and I learned, by his example, the power of giving trust and expecting employees to live up to it."

Tom Early hadn't chosen Joe without reason. He had observed Joe's work ethic from his days at Speers. "Before I knew it, I was kind of running the business," Joe says. "Mr. Early was a very good mentor. He had a way about him. He was a likable guy; we understood each other. He gave me a lot of latitude, and things worked out well for both parties." Joe was soon made manager.

Two years after Joe started at Early's, Tom hired Joe's brother, John, a survey engineer. "He had no connection to the business," Joe says, "but Mr. Early thought if John had the same work ethic as me, it would be a good fit."

Hard work and good fortune

Hard work was mandatory. Spencer Early recalls experiences working for his dad that have stuck with him in vivid detail–like packaging onion sets for eight hours a day upstairs in the old Idylwyld building during his high school years. Behind the store was the building that housed the machinery that cleaned and packaged grass seed. It was dusty, with the odd feral cat running around, and machines humming noisily. He remembers it as a great place for a kid to kick around in.

Spencer also recounts a memorable week working in the basement of the newly acquired, neighbouring United Grain Growers building. There were no special favours because you were the boss' kid. "There was one light bulb in the basement, with a bunch of bamboo canes covered in green dye," he recalls. "It was dark down there, kind of creepy, and similar to the area underneath the elevator where hobos would come from off the train to get work. Dad hired them in the spring to cut the eyes out of potatoes and bag them. He'd pay them, and then there'd be a different bunch at the next shift. You'd never see the same guys again. I worked with them. That was the job that needed doing."

Though he and his dad didn't have the closest relationship, Spencer truly admired his father for something the elder Early had that was well-documented–extraordinary good fortune. "He was the *luckiest* guy," Spencer says. "What a character. He once went on *The Price is Right* [the American television game show]. He just happened to be in California, and went into the audience for something to do.

The "creepy basement" of the United Grain Growers Building on Idylwyld, where Spencer worked for his dad as a high school student.

We have a copy of the videotape, and it's amazing to watch. He had never watched the show, didn't know how to play the game at all. He got called up, his first stroke of luck. Then, having no idea what to bid, he just fluked his way through to the end. He got in the final bid, and won the car. The tape is hilarious. I'm sure if they were to do a "top 10" of the craziest examples of someone winning who had no idea– Dad's would be at the top."

Joe recalls his brother, John's, first meeting with Tom Early at the Early house. They watched a hockey game, and Mr. Early had placed his friendly wager on the team with the longest odds. "John was flabbergasted when the team won," Joe says. "The odds were something unbelievable like 13 to 1. John said, 'I want to work for *that* guy!' And, of course, he ended up doing just that."

Spencer continued to work numerous odd jobs in Saskatoon, while he was in high school. "I wasn't spoiled because my dad owned a business," he says. "I had to work just as hard as anyone else." He had a job clerking at a drug store, and changing oil and tires at an Esso gas station.

As a young adult, Spencer actually pursued a path that led away from, rather than toward, the family business. He had the spirit of a nomad, and needed to satisfy his strong impulse to travel. He started by joining the Royal Officer Training Corps (ROTC). He went through Army and Navy training, including some parachute training with the airborne regiment in Edmonton. Through the ROTC education program, he studied engineering at the University of Saskatchewan and acquired his civil engineering degree in 1977.

L to R: John Bloski, Tom Early (wearing one of his infamous bolo ties) and Joe Bloski become partners in 1984.

After working a few jobs in Mexico and Calgary, Spencer finally settled down–at least temporarily. In 1978, he married Regina girl Jan Coffey, who shared his love of world travel. The couple lived in Saskatoon and Spencer worked as an engineer and consultant for a few years for a construction company. Then the travel bug hit again, and the couple spent two years traveling through the South Pacific, Asia, Australia and New Zealand.

One family becomes two

Early's Seed and Feed was an estate company, meaning that S.A. Early had willed the company to his five children. Of all the co-owner heirs, only Tom was active in the business. Though he didn't have majority ownership, he had the biggest individual share. Inheriting a shrewd business sense (and willingness to gamble) from his father, Tom made a

Specialty seed, like this golf grass at Saskatoon's Riverside Country Club, became a new successful line of business for Earlys in the mid-1980s.

decision in 1980 that would see ownership of the company extend beyond the Early family for the first time in six decades.

"John and I were running Early's Seed & Feed from the 1970s on–under Tom's guidance and leadership," Joe says. "The buildings on Idylwyld had become fatigued, and the Early family was aging–the brothers and sisters wanted to settle." Tom's solution was to form a new company, Early's Farm and Garden Centre in 1981, and to offer part ownership to the Bloskis. "He was the majority shareholder and John and I were minority shareholders," Joe says. "It had nothing to do with the previous company except that we bought out their seed inventory and some other equipment. What we didn't want, they sold off. We were only interested in doing retail."

Construction on a new location, on Lorne Avenue, started in 1982; and a move was planned for September. They confidently registered for a phone number associated with their goal (931.1982) but construction workers in Saskatoon went on strike and by December, Early's wasn't even close to moving in. Feeling pressure to be open before the spring rush, they pushed their contractor, Miners Construction, and finally opened the new 26,000 square foot retail store on February 23, 1983. The 70-year-old Early's Seed and Feed building closed downtown.

Moving on

Early's started at the new location with fewer than 15 employees, and, as Joe puts it, "It was a whole new ball game." In addition to more space and a retail environment, Tom Early had turned 65. He was easing out of the daily affairs of the company and looking toward retirement. He demonstrated his faith in the Bloski management team by staying in the background, and enjoying extended annual winter vacations in California.

It was also in 1983, that Joe's 20-year-old son, Derek, started working at Early's. He continued refereeing hockey–attaining "trainee" status in the NHL–while working at two jobs. Eventually, at age 26, Derek decided he didn't want to spend his life traveling and he came on full time with Early's as a management trainee. In 2009, he celebrated his 25th anniversary with the company.

Some of the most ambitious and risky entrepreneurial decision-making began at the outset of the new retail enterprise. Their first risk was betting on the expansion of the pet industry. "We got in on the threshold of the pet industry boom, and made that work," Joe says. Today, pet supplies account for nearly 40% of Early's sales revenues. Next, the company jumped aboard an explosion of opportunity in the golf course industry. Two new courses were being built in Saskatoon–the Willows and Moon Lake. Already established in the turf seed business, Early's ramped up their seed supply to accommodate the increase in demand. "We went from buying 50 bags of seed at a time to truckloads," Joe says. "It was a big risk, but one that had to be taken.

"Those kinds of risks gave us buying power," Joe says. "How much you buy governs the price you pay. We turned that risk, along with developing relationships with people at the courses, into getting the lion's share of the golf course business."

Prodigal son returns home

Tom's roving son, Spencer, approached his dad in July 1988, and asked to become involved in the family business. Tom asked Joe and John's opinion of bringing Spencer on board. At first, Joe and John weren't keen. "Really, at the time, we just weren't sure it was the right thing to do," Joe says. "Spencer didn't have a lot of experience in the industry." But Tom wanted to give his son a try.

"I think he felt he owed me a shot at it," Spencer says, "since I had come to him and asked. He was surprised. I hadn't shown much interest before–but people constantly asked me when I was going to go into the family business and, at some point, I couldn't see any reason not to."

So the namesake of founder S.A. joined the company–but he sure didn't walk in to the top job. "They put me in the warehouse, helping with shipping stuff," Spencer remembers. "No prestigious office job. Degree or not–you start in the back. Eventually, I worked my way into the rest of it."

The change was a big one for the Bloskis. First, there were work style and personality differences. Spencer is a very easy-going and more relaxed person; Joe is more driven and focused on business. "Joe's much more 'Type A' than I am," says Spencer. "He has a different style, and we're from different generations."

There was also the fact that the Bloskis had been successfully running and growing the business with Tom Early for many years, and weren't sure how the generational transition would work. "Each generation is different," says Spencer. "There's 'old school' which is *work your hardest*, then the next generation is a bit more relaxed–and today, the younger kids, coming up, are looking for what they think is a healthier balance between work and personal life. But, every generation brings something new and different to the business." And such was the case at Early's. In spite of all the unknowns of change, everyone adjusted, and the company continued to prosper.

In 1995, Spencer was made president, and Joe's second son, Kevin, joined Early's. Interested in building the golf-related business, Kevin brought his commerce education and considerable work experience to bear on expanding the turf business beyond serving golf course customers to include specialty grass projects like parks, other city landscaping projects and a variety of types of sports fields. "Kevin's done a great job of building an extensive network of relationships in the golf course industry," Spencer says. "He's a smart guy, really dedicated, and it has become almost a mini-business on its own."

To accommodate the higher volume needs of an expanding business, and to be competitive on price, Joe looked beyond the immediate vicinity for suppliers.

"We started buying direct from suppliers, particularly in the USA, which enabled us to be competitive to supply to golf courses, sod farms and other large professional users of turf grass and related products."

By the mid-1990s, the pet industry had become very specialized and sophisticated. Early's, having gotten in at the beginning of the boom, was comfortably positioned to continue its growth in that business, as well as turf. However, Joe was always looking for the next opportunity…and risk.

It came in the form of the garden and landscaping business. "Increased interest in the backyard living experience was a sign of the times," Joe says. "More families had two wage earners–which created some extra disposable income." Having learned from their experience with the pet sector, Early's risked making a sizable investment in inventory and advertising–banking on the growth associated with the slowly strengthening Saskatchewan economy. Again, their forward thinking paid off.

New century, new generations

On September 30, 2005, Tom Early died of respiratory disease. He had seen his father's company grow from a small feed and grain store to a multi-million dollar, diverse chain of retail stores. He had actively ensured that experienced and talented people were in place as his successors.

In his 43rd year, at Early's, Joe Bloski reflects on his career. Having been a life-long participant in community sports–and current vice-chair of the International Junior Hockey Championships scheduled for 2010 in Saskatoon–Joe sees many parallels between the role of an entrepreneur and company leader and the role of a coach or captain of a sports team. "I heard Russ Jackson [former Saskatchewan Roughriders quarterback] speak recently. He said, 'Nothing worthwhile comes easy. It takes commitment and hard work. There's no magic.' He was talking about success in sports, of course, but it's also true in business, and in life," Joe says. "Nobody owes you a living and, ultimately, everyone on the team still has to buy in to the coach's philosophy. It's the same in business."

The calculated risk-taking philosophy of S.A. and Tom Early is very much part of the growth of the modern-day company. Joe says, "Our experience has shown us that you have to recognize opportunity when it appears, and know when to exploit it. It's only an opportunity if you take advantage of it."

In Spencer's mind, the biggest turning point of the second half of the company's history was the move to the large Lorne Avenue retail space–an expansion that likely wouldn't have happened without the Bloski's willingness to take on its management. "Dad wasn't willing to make that move if they'd said no," says Spencer. "It's possible the company wouldn't even have gone on after that point."

When asked about the future of Early's, both Spencer and Joe say, "You never know…" For personal and family reasons, the Bloski's sold their portion of the business back to the Early family in 2001. Nonetheless, Early's Farm and Garden Centre continues as a multi-family, multi-generational business. Joe's sons, Kevin and Derek, have children, and Spencer's two grown children, Andrea and John, may eventually be interested in working in the business. But both fathers want their children and

Earlys moved to its current location on Lorne Avenue in 1983.

grandchildren to determine their own futures. Both Joe and Spencer talk a great deal about the quality (and longevity) of the family of Early staff members, whose average length of employment is 10 years. Continuing on "…isn't only about money," Spencer says. "It's more about what's good for business, and the quality of life for our staff, that's a huge factor. Our decisions affect their lives.

"You can talk about the management and, of course it's important that it's good; but the *staff* knows this company, inside and out, and is loyal and really is a family," Spencer says.

Long-time advocates of buying locally to preserve jobs in the community, Spencer and Jan have also invested in other businesses, including hotel developments, with the caveat that employees are hired from the community.

At the end of the day, like many others in his position, the third-generation Early joins his colleague Joe Bloski in paying his respects to his father and grandfather–whose visions continue to guide the company today.

"I still think the original work they did was the real entrepreneurship," Spencer says. "We're doing the maintenance, and doing a decent job of it, but they were the ones that built something from nothing."

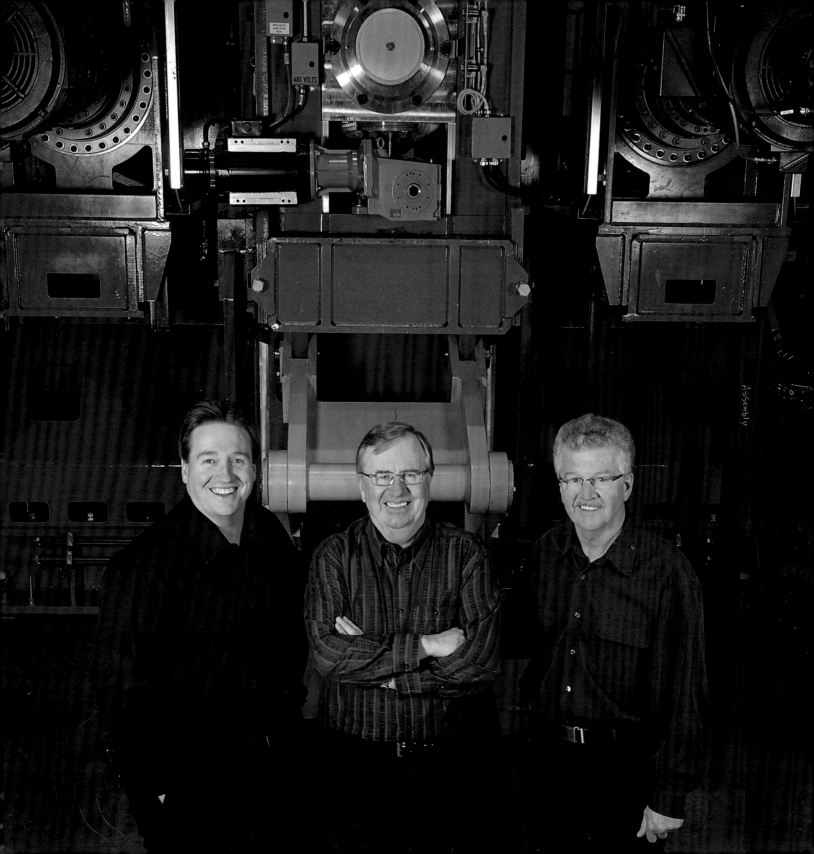

Gavin Semple
Dreaming big

"Scarcity, when you're a kid, isn't a bad thing–it causes you to dream."
– Gavin Semple

There's something about starting with nothing that fuels imagination and desire, and nobody embodies that drive more than Brandt Industries Ltd. President Gavin Semple.

"I think of my own history–and this is true of a lot of people who are entrepreneurs or inventors," Semple says, "I was born and raised on a farm 18 miles north of Regina, across the road from Piapot First Nation. My dad, John Semple, was 24 years older than my mother. There were six kids in our family. My dad was a successful farmer, but you wouldn't know it–we had no central heating system, no running water, no electricity and no conveniences." This was common for other farm families in the area.

On the Semple farm, developing a strong work ethic wasn't an option. "We worked hard. Our dad was a determined Scotsman. One word we couldn't say was 'can't.' We never did–we would've been embarrassed to say it." Semple shakes his head at the differences today, no matter how cliché the story of "how things used to be" may sound. "It would be - 37°C, the coldest day of the year, and we'd go to school with the horse and sleigh. We never stayed home because of the weather; that would be shirking our responsibility. Today, it gets cold and the buses don't run; the kids don't go to school."

Without external media, like television, to present images of the world, the Semple kids had to have active imaginations. "I think when a kid is very young–eight or nine–that's when the seeds are sown," Semple says. "We had to dream."

Shaun, Gavin and Jim Semple in front of one of many unique pipe handling projects designed at Brandt Engineered Products Ltd.

Working as a team from childhood, young Gavin holds the plow, while brother, Jim, leads the horse, in 1958.

Learning from the ground up

If you wanted something, you worked out a way to make the money to buy it yourself. Gavin remembers when he and brother Jim helped the youngest brother Jack figure out a way to get his first guitar. "When he was about nine, Jack wanted to play guitar," Gavin recalls. "We cut out a picture of a guitar and an amp from the Sears catalogue, and put it up on the door in his bedroom. We told him if he did his chores every day, he could earn a dollar a day. By March, several months later, he'd earned enough to buy it. He came home one day, and we had the guitar and amp for him. He picked up that guitar and hasn't set it down since."

Jack Semple is now a much-admired, popular and award-winning recording artist with a reputation far beyond Saskatchewan's borders. Meanwhile, his big brothers Jim and Gavin shared a different dream– that of business…big business.

Being raised on a farm taught the Semple kids to see how hard work made something from nothing. "You learn to relate the sowing to the harvest," Gavin says. "You see it, live, from the time you're little. You learn, first-hand, that when you work hard, you get a result at the end of the process."

Because there was no school bus system, 14-year-old Gavin moved to Regina to go to high school. He lived in the dormitory at Luther College, and finished high school at age 18, in 1963. His father died suddenly in March 1964, leaving Gavin's mother to raise the five children still at home, and to run a good-sized farm with 125 head of cattle. There was no question what Gavin would do. "It happened suddenly, so we took the responsibility to manage the farm and help out," he says. Gavin worked with his older brother Bill to run the farm.

Gavin married Annette Marcotte in 1966, and they lived on the farm. To supplement their farm income, Annette commuted to Regina to work at SaskTel in the accounting department, and Gavin began a sales career. A natural "people person," Gavin quickly learned he could excel at sales, and sell he did–everything from vacuums to duck decoys to insurance and even, he reluctantly admits, cosmetics.

But the idealistic young man had a dream, to make more money. He devoured every kind of motivational material he could get his hands on, from books to tapes to workshops and courses. "I read Dr. Napoleon Hill's *Think and Grow Rich* and learned Earl Nightingale's *Fundamentals of Success*. I discovered I had an insatiable appetite for knowledge about successful people and what made them successful," he says.

At age 27, in 1972, Gavin learned about an opening for a sales position at Brandt Machine and Manufacturing Ltd., a company started by electrical contractor, Abram Peter Brandt, in 1932. Originally Brandt Electric, the company had more than four decades of experience designing and building innovative agricultural equipment like cultivators and crop dusters–and one of the first grain augers available in Canada.

Gavin pulled up in front of Brandt in a blue 1961 Pontiac, for which he'd paid $300, and was hired the same day as a territory salesman. He says all of his net worth was in that blue Pontiac. He started selling agricultural, trenching and golf course equipment in the Southwest Region of Saskatchewan. Within a year, he was promoted to sales manager.

"By the time I came to Brandt, I was so excited," he says. "I thought, 'I'm selling legitimate stuff that people really *need*.' Every week, I had a stack of sales orders. As sales manager, I hired other young people I could motivate and teach. I built an energized team, and the company took off."

Sales skyrocketed five fold in four years, from $1 million to $5 million.

In 1976, at age 31, Gavin became president and general manager. He purchased 15% of the company's shares, and parlayed that into a majority shareholder position by 1982.

Among the concepts he learned early on, were setting clear goals, and having a concrete plan with timelines. "So you have a *reason* for doing what you're doing," he says. "I focused on the service side. If I put enough into the service side–finding out a customer's needs and fulfilling those needs–life will balance it on the rewards side."

Like father, like son

In 1984, Gavin's 17-year-old son Shaun joined Brandt. "Shaun was born to be in business," his father says. "He had a great business head from the beginning. He said to me, 'I want a sales job–I'll sell the machine shop services.' We had never done this before, so I felt like I was throwing him to the wolves."

But Gavin needn't have worried. Even though, like his father, Shaun possessed the natural people skills so requisite to success in sales, nobody predicted how quickly he'd make his mark. "We had tried to do business in the past with a large industrial customer," Gavin says. "They were a very big player, but we hadn't had much success. When Shaun said he wanted to try to get their business, the machine shop people were naturally very skeptical–because of Shaun's age and because we had never been successful with that customer. Shaun ran with it, and got their business. That company, today, is one of our largest customers."

Shaun tells the story of that day: "I had my grade 12 when I came into the business. At that time,

Gavin as a child on the family farm, north of Regina.

43

A younger Gavin, during his early days as a salesman in the 1980s.

the agriculture industry was a tough place to be. We'd always done custom manufacturing outside of agriculture, but it was very small. One day, Dad said, 'Here's a pick up truck, here's a customer list—go see what you can do.' I had no training, no experience—he just threw me in the truck with a list of customers and instructions to see what I could sell.

"Previously, we'd done about $200 of business with this large customer—that was it. I looked at the customer list, and thought, 'Gee, they're a pretty big business—maybe I should call on them.' On that Friday afternoon, I drove out at 4 p.m., which you'd think wouldn't be the best time to call on a customer. I walked up to the security gate and asked to see the manufacturing manager. They called the vice president of manufacturing. Well, he saw me right away. He said, 'Funny you called. Today's the last day for our machine shop. We're going to be contracting it all out. Come back on Monday and see this guy.'"

Driving back after that fortuitous meeting, Shaun says he felt great. "I was thinking, we had five machinists and one welder in our custom shop, and I'd just learned that they had about 25 machinists. And they were now going to contract out all that work. It was huge."

Starting from the bottom and working his way up like his father, Shaun's role grew with his success. He started in sales of custom machining and fabrication, moved on to other sales positions and became manufacturing manager. He worked in "every department in the company," his dad says.

In 1992, Shaun became president of Brandt Tractor Ltd., the largest of the five companies in the Brandt Group.

Divide and conquer

Gavin's brother, Jim, had joined Brandt in 1986, as machine shop manager. By then, business was "busting at the seams." Different business lines (turf and trenching, custom machining, agricultural products, and distribution) were all taking off, and Gavin, Jim and Shaun were having difficulty staying focused. "We were growing, all under one roof. But we were a jack of all trades, master of none," Gavin says.[1] It was becoming hard for them to maintain focus on their business, because they weren't really sure what the business was.

The company was sitting at about $9 million in sales revenue, and the Semples decided it was time for Brandt Industries to *really* grow.

Operating on the notion that each business needed specialized attention to grow, they made a landmark decision to separate all the business divisions into separate companies.

"We wanted to shelter ourselves from the ups and downs of the agriculture industry—things can go from great to not good in a hurry," Gavin says. "And it has proved, over and over again, to have been a very good decision. Even today, we have staying power. We continue to thrive in the down times, because one

The Brandt Tractor division, run by Gavin's son, Shaun.

business will be strong and be able to support continuing development in another. So, we never have to cut back on valuable research and development, for example, because we can afford to continue to invest."

At the time, however, the decision required a massive leap of faith. "Financial statements look good when you're driving a lot of money through a small company," Gavin says. "Dividing the enterprise into separate businesses with separate financial statements gave us clear visibility into the viability of each business, but we were taking a risk."

The first business to leave the nest was the turf and trenching division. Shaun managed the move to Winnipeg Street and Ross Avenue in Regina. He had to buy a building and land, staff the operation and create new departments–sales, service, accounting, and others. The fledgling company had to become self-reliant, build its own systems and make a go of it on its own merits. The new division was profitable in 1989, its first year of operation.

As often happens in entrepreneurial activity, opportunity arises when you're working on some-

thing else. While the dividing up of the business was occurring, the now 26-year-old Shaun read an ad in the paper one day that would lead to an historic move in 1992.

Gavin says, "John Deere was looking for a dealer for construction and forestry equipment. Shaun sought direction from various sources and, despite advice to the contrary, was determined that he could succeed as a specialized John Deere dealer."

"Even Dad wasn't sure," Shaun remembers. "He often said of that decision, 'We said no [to the idea] nine times and yes 10 times.'" In another example of his perseverance in entrepreneurism, Shaun went forward in creating the new line of business for Brandt. "I was dead set that we were going to do it. If others could do it, so could we. Today, we have the largest John Deere dealership network in the world."

Entrepreneurs out there, take heed: "You have to believe you can do it–and you have to have a vision and strategy," Shaun says. "Not every business will give you the same kind of returns, but if you don't have those two things, you're not going to be successful."

45

Brandt Tractor was awarded the Saskatchewan territory but, as Gavin recalls, they were on a tight deadline. "They told us we had only six weeks to open. We had no John Deere experience, no people, no place of business. But we opened one dealership in Regina in six weeks and a second dealership, a month later, in Saskatoon. Shaun adds, "It proves that anything is possible, no matter what anyone tells you along the way. When someone tells me I can't do something, that's my motivator."

Growing like wildfire, by 1995 Brandt Tractor had merged with a Manitoba dealer and purchased dealerships in Calgary and Red Deer. In 1999, they added dealerships in Edmonton, Grand Prairie, and Fort McMurray. Then they moved into British Columbia, where they bought 13 dealerships from the Guinness Company in the UK. Brandt Tractor now has the largest John Deere dealership network in the world. With 850 employees, it currently makes up the biggest part of the Brandt Group of Companies.

Meanwhile, the Semples were continuing the re-visioning of Brandt into separate, focused, divisions–set up as individual companies. The custom machining and fabrication shop expanded in 1994, headed up by Jim Semple, and became its own company, Brandt Custom Machining and Fabrication. "We took a risk, getting 50,000 square feet when we'd been working out of 5,000," Gavin says. "We wondered how we'd ever fill up that space. The costs were going to be much higher than what we were accustomed to, so it led to the usual question, 'Can we make this pay, or are we expanding beyond our capability and our ability to make it work?'"

The answer wasn't long in coming. "We bit the bullet and we bought the 50,000 square foot building. We believed in the management and the employees in that division. In no time, we were at capacity and we have expanded six times since, now comprising 114,000 square feet."

In 1998, another creation of the "division strategy," Brandt Agricultural Products Ltd., moved into a 110,000 square foot building to service a growing domestic and international market for agricultural equipment. This company now employs 200 people and ships products around the globe.

The strategy of specializing has been an enormous success. Gavin has built Brandt on many of the "people" strategies he learned back in his sales training days. Strategic goals were tied to pay structures to create a sense of ownership and entrepreneurship in each of the companies. "We have a lot of entrepreneurs within the companies," he says. "We have metrics or goals within each department and managers are compensated on achievement of metrics. In this way, they start to view their department, or division, as their own business."

46   Brandt Group of Companies' head office in Regina.

The "road-railer" is an exciting, innovative tool for the railroad industry that Brandt sells to a world-wide market.

The 'road-railer'

While all this restructuring was going on, opportunity struck in the form of innovation in 1991.

"Rail line abandonment was happening in Saskatchewan," Gavin recalls. "Grain transport was switching to highway systems, which was a growing concern to the provincial government. The question was, 'What can be done to keep grain hauling on rail and save the deteriorating road system?' The government wanted to facilitate the development of shortline rail companies, but you couldn't have a locomotive on every branch line."

The Department of Highways came up with the idea of taking a semi-tractor and putting retractable rail running gear on it, so that it could run on both the road system and the rail system. The modified highway tractor could pull 15 100-ton grain cars. So if you had two towns 100 miles apart, the road railer (also known as the Brandt Power Unit) could move from one branch line to another on the road system and then go onto track, hook onto the train cars and pull them down the tracks to the next town.

The government tendered the building of a prototype and Brandt was the successful bidder. "They knew of our custom machining and manufacturing division and came to us," Gavin says. "We had been successful in the past in building specialized equipment, so we were given the opportunity to manufacture this unique locomotive. We started working with the Department of Highways on the project."

High-capacity belt conveyor used for conveying a variety of agricultural products including wheat and peas.

As Brandt began to build the prototype, Jim thought there might be more commercial potential than just the provincial government project, so Gavin went to the government and negotiated the manufacturing and marketing rights in a partnership with them. They formed a new company (Brandt Road Rail Corporation), and the Brandt Power Unit was born. The first one was sold to the Canadian National railroad (CN).

Brandt bought the patents from the government, and has now developed a full line of rail maintenance equipment for shortline rail companies, Class 1 railways and transit systems in major American cities. "All of the Class 1 railways have Brandt Power Units now," Gavin says.

Export sales comprise most of the company's revenues, but it was the idea of the road railers,

nurtured for 10 years before it really caught on, that really excites Gavin. Faith in the idea's potential was necessary long before it was accepted in the market place. "We kept after it and kept after it," Gavin says. "And our specialization approach really paid off. The Brandt Power Unit is a unique product in the world, with a long sales cycle, and the people in that division are completely dedicated to it. Now we sell it across North America, and in Australia, Venezuela and Mexico."

Over the years, Brandt engineers developed a reputation for building whatever a customer wanted. "We have built potato-handling systems for McCain Foods and Simplot," Gavin says. "And we built the boom for the largest dragline at the Estevan coal mine."

Now called Brandt Engineered Products Ltd., the company has evolved into a global manufacturer of automated pipe and steel handling and testing systems and rail maintenance equipment.

Giving back

In the midst of all this success ($900 million in sales in 2008), the Semples and Brandt have been as vigilant about giving back to their community as they have been about running their business. In addition to the major sponsorships and donations to the Brandt Centre, Luther College, the United Way and many other worthwhile causes, Gavin serves on numerous community and business organizations. In 2008, he was named deputy chair of the board of Enterprise Saskatchewan, the provincial government's department devoted to supporting the province's economic growth. As the business-appointed representative, Gavin works with others in sectors like agriculture, energy, cooperatives, labour, aboriginal, post secondary education and municipalities in order to achieve Premier Brad Wall's vision of sustained growth and prosperity.

"He's asked us to try to engage everyone to answer the question 'What does the province need to do to sustain growth?'" Gavin says. "Part of the reason we're doing well in Saskatchewan is because resource commodities are doing well. But what do we need for long-term prosperity?"

The work of the board has included creating 18 sector teams to identify the barriers to growth, where the opportunities are, and what the government needs to do to help make it happen. "We've made some progress. Some recommendations to government have already been implemented," Gavin says. "Things like tax reduction and regulatory modernization." While there's much more to do, he is hopeful and positive about the potential for Saskatchewan sectors and government to work together to build on the recent "Saskaboom" and ensure long-term sustainability.

Secrets of success

When asked what ideas he believes are key for today's young entrepreneurs, Gavin says, "The best advice I could give is to study others who've done it before you. Learn from people's experience–what it's like to be an entrepreneur–the pluses and minuses." And, he adds, "If you want to do it, you have to believe in yourself. You don't have to have all the answers to start–you can't. Have faith, believe in yourself, and go for it."

Resiliency is another key. "You're going to be knocked down–lots of times. You have to get up and keep fighting. There are lots of unexpected surprises when you're trying to establish your own business. You have to be persistent, and have the attitude of never giving up. If you really do that, you'll find all the answers. You cannot defeat someone who won't quit."

He also encourages would-be entrepreneurs to research and plan on the business side; to find out everything they can from a marketing perspective. Questions, he says, like: Is there a need? How big is the market? Why will they buy from you and not someone else?

Speaking at an Enterprise Saskatchewan staff luncheon on change and corporate values in 2008, Gavin emphasized the need for ensuring that change happens, no matter what. "In manufacturing, you get comfortable developing the same products that are very successful. There can be a tendency not to change or develop the next model, for a variety of reasons. You don't want to risk cannibalizing sales of your existing products, they are great products–so, *success* can be a deterrent to more success. Put another way, good is the enemy of great."

To keep ahead of the game, Gavin says you need to change before competitors do. And risk is inherent. "You can't wait until it's obvious to everybody what the situation is–because by that time, the train has left the station."[2]

"If there's a secret to it all–and there's not just one–the single most important thing is finding the right people. Develop the right culture, compensate people well, enjoy the people part of it," he says. "I attribute Brandt's success over the years to the company's focus on attracting and retaining a team of highly motivated, talented, people who execute the

Many Canadian farmers recall having this original grain auger invented by Peter Brandt.

company's strategy of diversification through specialized business units." This strategy has taken Brandt from "a small, $1 million dollar company to the largest private company in Saskatchewan (approaching $1 billion in revenues)."

Gavin says that he is a major proponent of learning sales skills–and not just for the obvious reasons. "Some of those sales skills you learn along the way, the people aspects of the business, stand you in good stead when you get into management positions. Good sales people have to be good listeners, not just good talkers," he cautions. "If you're good at listening, and try to understand what the needs of the customer are, you will succeed in selling." Being a good listener is also an important trait in management and other leadership positions.

In fact, Semple says, successful business people never really stop selling–their company, their product or service, or themselves. "In reality, we're selling all the time. You're either doing a good job of it, or a poor job," he says. "You're in the business of trying to persuade people to do the things you want done to move the organization ahead. You can call that whatever you like but, at the end of the day, I think it's selling your vision of where you want to go."

Success has its personal side, too. "My success is due to the support of a lot of people, not the least of whom are my family," Gavin says. In addition to his son and brother, who work in the business, his daughter Juanita works in the company's human resources department–attracting and developing the company's most valued assets, the employees. Gavin has been married to Annette since 1966, and is quick to credit her unwavering support over those many years as a significant key to his success.

Founder laid groundwork for innovation

And how does Gavin see the legacy of founder, Peter Brandt, extending into today's global enterprise?

One word–innovation.

"I didn't know Mr. Brandt, but the one product that we still manufacture today is the Brandt grain auger, which he pioneered in Western Canada," Gavin says. "In the 1940s, when Mr. Brandt developed this product, it was deemed very innovative. He was also very innovative in everything he manufactured in the company at that time. Innovation remains a core value for us today."

Brandt and the Semples have been the recipients of numerous awards over the years. Among them, Brandt has been named a Platinum Member of Canada's 50 Best Managed Companies for eight consecutive years (2000-08). Both Gavin (1994) and Shaun (1999) have received the Entrepreneur of the Year Award. Shaun was named one of "Canada's Top 40 under 40" by the Toronto Globe & Mail in 2000, and was the 2006 ABEX Business Leader of the Year. Gavin has been inducted into both the Canadian Professional Sales Hall of Fame (2004) and the Canadian Manufacturers Hall of Fame (2009). In 2008, he received the Saskatchewan Order of Merit, a prestigious recognition of excellence, achievement and contributions to the social, cultural and economic well being of the province and its residents. The Order recognizes individuals who have made their mark in such areas as the arts, agriculture, business and industry, community leadership, the occupations or professions, public service, research, and volunteer service. It takes precedence over all other provincial honours and awards.[3]

Gavin, Jim and Shaun Semple had a big dream, and they're still living it.

And, just so you know–little brother, Jack, is doing pretty darned well, too.

Founder Peter Abram Brandt in 1930.

George & Wendy Morris
Doing what has to be done

The little girl cherished breakfast time with her father before he went to work. It was rare to have his undivided attention—for it to be just the two of them. Sadly, her mother was ill. She was going through undiagnosed and untreated depression, a typical scenario for many women through the 1950s. The girl's father was often away because of his business, and her siblings were in school.

That little girl was Wendy Morris, who would grow up to become president of the company her father had started in 1921. She remembers how she was called at a young age to the task of responsibility. "I would get up in the morning, in my p.j.'s and, every day, his last words upon leaving for work were: 'Now, be a good girl, Wendy, and look after your mother while I'm gone.' I would sit outside her bedroom and play with my toys until she got up. Being quiet and not upsetting her was my idea of looking after her. I tried to help in any way she would let me. I knew I was expected to be responsible, so that's what I was. Later in life, when someone had to take responsibility, I always did."

When she was 20, Wendy accepted responsibility for her mentally ill brother, whose erratic behaviour was causing threatening situations at home. "I had to move him out of the house," she says. "Someone had to make that decision for my parents, because they didn't want to."

She would always do what needed doing, and would try to live all the values of her father, George Morris. This sense of duty would also have enormous impact, in ways she could never imagine, on her life, and on the agricultural implement company that grew from her father's garage in the village of Bangor.

Wendy Morris brought Morris Industries back into competitive status in the '90s by returning to her father's simple principle of listening to the customer, and applying it to the design of practical agricultural implements like this Morris 8370 Air Cart.

Five-year-old Wendy with her father, George, in 1959.

Searching for a new home

The story of the Morris family starts with the struggle of their disenfranchised Welsh forebears. Oppression of Welsh farmers in the mid-1800s by English landlords resulted in poverty and a dampening of cultural identity, causing many to dream of starting over in another place. In 1865, a small group of colonists headed for South America, and a region called "Patagonia."

Surviving many hardships in their first winter, the colonists became successful farmers, but their dream of a fully independent Welsh state wouldn't come true. In 1895, Welsh immigrants, Clara Davies and Robert Morris, met. They were married in Trelew, Patagonia, in 1896.

Unfortunately, the Argentinean government began exhibiting many of the same oppressive behaviors of the British, and the Welsh found themselves again looking for a new home.

True North, strong and free

The Canadian government was looking for settlers for the Prairies, and had been in touch with the Patagonia Welsh, whom they called "splendidly adapted for life in a new country."[1] An advance party of 30 left Patagonia in 1902, among them, the Morris family– Robert, Clara and their two children, Bill and Emma.

The trip must have been tough for Clara Morris, who was eight months pregnant with son, Hugh. Though winters were harsh, the Welsh had been through worse. Soon after arriving, Robert built a log house for the family, which they moved into in the fall of 1903. Their fourth child, George Henry Morris, was born on July 1, 1904. They would eventually have five more children.

Improving farming methods and machinery

In 1901, the area that is now Saskatchewan had 1.1 million acres of broken ground, 655,000 acres of which was in crop.[2] This was all done with horse and man "power." Tillage practices included plowing, packing, discing and harrowing. The horses pulled the implement and the farmer either rode or walked behind. Steam-powered threshing machines came into use early in the century, and, then, the self-propelled stream traction engine.

In the first 20 years of the new century, farmers began recognizing the importance of moisture conservation, weed control and wind erosion, and "summer fallowing" was discovered, by accident, in the Indian Head area.[3]

The Dust Bowl of the Dirty Thirties forced other changes to happen. The plow, for instance, was replaced by cultivators, which worked the soil, but left the surface undisturbed, thereby reducing the wind erosion of topsoil. The cable and rod weeder, which worked below the soil surface, were also invented, and ushered in the era in which a young George Morris would turn his inventive mind, his unstoppable problem-solving focus and his dogged determination to the task of making things better for prairie farmers.

George grows up

George was schooled from age seven (in 1911) to age 13. As author Dick deRyk wrote: "By today's standards he would be considered illiterate, but that didn't bother him. In later life he would say he was more concerned about the 'educated illiterate.'"[4] He was a pleasant, average student. He wasn't a complainer. He was happy, funny, helpful to others and a good sport.

But George's most characteristic trait was his inventiveness. At age 11, he came to school with a threshing machine he'd built. It maneuvered on solid wood wheels, connected by an iron axle made by his dad. On that, was a box, and inside, was a piece of old fanning belt. On the side of the box, was a handle connected to a series of wheels and belts. The kids used it to play "farmer." They turned its handle to collect up leaves, pretending they were straw piles.[5]

George's mechanical prowess increased as he grew up. In 1924, at the suggestion of his father, George went to Winnipeg to learn the motor mechanic trade. He completed a four-month course at a trade school, and returned to Bangor in time for the harvest. The next spring, at only 20 years old, he began his career as a garage owner.

The fix-it man

Everyone in town knew George Morris could fix anything, and his garage became a centre of business activity: selling gasoline to farmers in glass bottles from the two pumps out front, stocking items like battery-operated radios and providing services like gravel-hauling. In 1927, he added the Cockshutt equipment line to his inventory. Eventually, there was a demand for generators, and George sold gasoline-powered ones and windmills. To people who didn't have electricity, he sold coal oil refrigerators and freezers, hand-cranked cream separators and washing machines with gas motors. In fact, determined to make it through the Depression, George sold any-thing for which there was a demand.

George's parents, Clara and Robert Morris, in Patagonia in the 1890s.

George also built himself tools as he needed them. The Bangor garage would be the birthplace of the farm implement that George would become best known for, though it would be 30 years before it would be mass produced.

The rod weeder

In 1901, Henry Wolfe, a farmer near Cheney, Washington, purportedly invented the rod weeder–an implement described as a "wheeled carriage carrying a shaft or rod adapted to be moved below the surface of the ground and with means to rotate the rod."[6] By moving the rod backwards, against the direction the rod weeder was moving, weeds would be pulled out and left on the soil to die.

With concerns about soil erosion, the implement quickly became popular, and many variations sprang up. In 1929, a progressive farmer from the original group of Patagonia Welsh settlers, John Lloyd Thomas, told George that the Cheney weeder he'd bought did a "dandy job" of weeding, but wouldn't stand up to the stony fields of the prairies. When pulling through fields, the rod would bend or break when it hit a large stone.[7]

George's mind went to work, and it wasn't long before he had a solution: a rod assembly that would *lift* to travel over stones, and then lower itself back into the ground to continue weeding. His theory was to have the rod assembly stretch a spring as it moved back to "trip" over a stone. Once past the stone, the spring would snap back, and cause the rod to go back down into the soil.

As was his practice, he built a small-scale model out of cardboard, which proved that his "trip"

mechanism would work. The first design worked well, but the machine was too complicated and, as a result, too expensive. He tried to sell the design from 1929 to 1932, but no major manufacturers were interested. In the winter of 1929-30, George redesigned it, making it simpler and cheaper. Though the all-steel construction made his rod weeder still slightly more expensive, other changes had lowered it into an acceptable price range.

Though he had to keep his faith in his machine for a long time, eventually, through an ad in the Western Producer, he sold his first Morris Rod Weeder. He had to borrow the $1,000 to build it. (He would eventually buy it back, in 1951, and donate it to the Western Development Museum in Yorkton, where it remains today.)

Continuing to advance his design, George tested improvements continuously with area farmers–under the severest conditions he could muster. This became a life-long practice in product development for George and those in his company. He was successful in acquiring a patent on his improved invention in April 1932. With no interest from manufacturers and sales starting, George connected with a machine shop owner in Portage la Prairie, Manitoba, and began manufacturing them himself.

George improved on the rod weeder with an ingenious "trip" device that kept the rod from breaking when it hit stones in the field.

The Morris Garage in Bangor (1930s). The building was both work and home to George and his helper.

During this time, at the age of 31, George married Helen Mary McDougall, eight years his junior. The two had known each other all their lives. They moved into Bangor, renting a home they would later purchase on Main Street–across from the Morris Garage. The business continued to grow, and George continued to invent, innovate and listen to the needs of his growing customer base. Meanwhile, their first daughter, Evelyn, was born in 1940, and Adeleine and Vernon followed a few years later.

In 1938, born of an informal and ongoing sense of community helpfulness, George organized the Bangor Co-op.

Doing the right thing, at the right time

By the late 1940s, George's business had literally outgrown Bangor–there was still no electricity in the village, and no more places for employees to live. In 1946, George joined up with Jack Baron, a successful blacksmith, and the two became partners in invention for 34 years. In 1948, he and Helen moved their family and business to Yorkton. Along with his employees, he built the 60-foot by 80-foot building himself. The official opening was in June 1949. The company was renamed the Morris Rod Weeder & Equipment Company. He continued to sell equipment, but the space was designed to also accommodate design and development of new equipment.

Development began immediately. A snow blower and a left-hand swather were the first, built to attach to the Allis Chalmers tractors George sold. In 1952, he was named Allis Chalmers' Canadian dealer with the highest sales. His total sales that year were $250,000. The invention of the "Morris Seed-Rite," an ingenious

implement that seeded, weeded and packed in one operation, was the next big hit.

When asked for the secret of his success, George said, "Doing the right thing at the right time."

He knew the right thing, and the right time, because he was so in tune with the needs of his community. "A lot of people ask me how many engineers we have," George once said. "I always answer that we have thousands of them. All of our customers who have suggestions are engineers."

George never tried to create a demand for a product, as is often the case today. "I'm not about to build something and then tell people they need it," he said. "We don't build things on speculation. If the need and the want is there for a machine, we'll fill it."[8]

Through the 1950s, George kept trying to sell the Morris Rod Weeder to implement manufacturers. He knew there was potential for the machine in the American Northern Plains states and, eventually, set up dealers in North Dakota, Montana and Alberta.

Even when he started making money, he saw no need to increase his spending beyond what was logical and necessary. The family moved to a slightly larger home in 1949 which, with some additions, would be their home for 40 years. In 1949, Raymond was born. Wendy, the youngest, came along in 1954.

In 1973, the size of the York Road Yorkton plant doubled to 117,000 square feet.

George was financially conservative in business, as well. He never borrowed more than 50% of the money needed for a new project. Because of this, the company was able to keep a high credit rating, even during the bad years suffered by implement makers in the 1980s.

In 1959, George decided to build a factory on York Road, in Yorkton, and it was a major turning point in the company and family's life. There was no looking back after the new plant opened in 1960. Morris continued to expand for the next 18 years.

Like father, like daughters

Perhaps the two closest relationships George had with his children were with Adeleine and Wendy. The older of the two, Adeleine, spent a lot of time with her father during her recovery from polio, which she contracted during the 1952 epidemic. During this time, her father drove her to Regina once a month to get therapy, and helped her with her physiotherapy at home, twice a day, for four years.

By the time Wendy reached school age, her sisters had left home. George would take her along with him for a treat on Sundays after church, and then to the shop. Wendy later said, "Whatever he did there, I'm not too sure, but I spent my time climbing on the tractors and being bored until we came home for supper."[9]

In her early 20s Wendy told her dad that there should be a woman working on the factory floor at the plant. George agreed. "He was very confident that a woman would do as good a job or better," Wendy said.[10] So, regardless of resistance in the male-only workplace, Wendy became the first woman to work on the Morris production line, in the drill department, over a summer break from university.

All the Morris girls were influenced by their mother, Helen, who kept up with news on feminism, and felt that women had been taken advantage of by society for long enough. All three became independent women who chose to keep their maiden names for life, and Adeleine is a feminist activist.

After studying journalism, at Ryerson, becoming a journalist and working as a communications officer, Adeleine was appointed president of Morris in 1986–a job she would hold for five years.

It would be Wendy, though, who would step in when things got toughest and carry on her father's reputation and name–a job that would cost her great personal sacrifice, but would also dramatically enrich her life.

When the going gets rough

"I told my dad when I was a teenager that I would *never* work for him," Wendy, says. "He had a smile on his face, and just said, 'that's fine, Wendy.' Even though I did work there for a while, between university terms, I needed to be far away from Morris. In the '70s, when company was large and father was well known, I wanted to get out of the province–just to be myself."

Wendy shared her feelings with George. "I told him, 'It's so hard to be your daughter–to fill your shoes.' He looked at me, with concern, and said, 'Well, Wendy, we should all just do the best we can.'"

Long an advocate for the use of non-chemical methods for improved health, George was the one who got Wendy interested in nutrition. "When he had his stroke,[11] he became very interested in alternative treatments–eating healthy food, and lowering his cholesterol," Wendy says. "Many of the things Dad looked at were considered quackery, but he was not the kind of person who was going to be discouraged by the so-called *authorities* telling him he wasn't right. If it looked right to him, he was going to stick with it, and that has probably been responsible for 99% of his success. Maybe you can say that for all entrepreneurs."[12]

"He suggested that nutrition would be a very good area for me to go into, if I was interested. I had done well in math and science in school, and actually decided that it would appeal to me."

So, Wendy went her own way. In 1978, she married John Wach in Edmonton after graduating with a bachelor's degree from the University of Alberta and interning at the U of A hospital as a dietician.

But she wasn't destined to become a nutritionist. She moved back to Saskatchewan with John, who started a Kindersley Dodge dealership with a partner in 1983. Nutritionist jobs weren't available anywhere near Kindersley, so Wendy went to work at the dealership, handling the books.

In the late 1980s, Wendy had no idea she would end up working for her dad's company one day. Raising two children, Bryce and Katherine (both named for Welsh ancestors), and working with her husband in Kindersley, there was no reason to think she would. But fate intervened–Dodge stopped making an extended cab truck, while Ford and GM continued, which dramatically affected the truck sales in their rural dealership. John decided to sell used vehicles instead.

Then, in 1991, Wendy got a call from her older sister, Adeleine, who had been president at Morris for five years.

"I've had enough," Adeleine told her sister. Adeleine had been hired by a management firm in 1982 to professionalize management and procedures at Morris, and to address a pressing economic need for stringent reductions of facilities and staff. She was exhausted and dejected by the layoffs and plant closures that she'd had to implement to get the company through the low economic times.

To make matters worse, in 1989, at age 85, George Morris had a third and fatal stroke. He was buried in the Llewelyn Cemetery, just down the hill from the headstones bearing the names of his pioneer ancestors, and an entrepreneurial era ended.

L to R: Ray, Helen, Wendy, George and Vernon. Standing in back are Evelyn and Adeleine.

There's work to do

"Adeleine decided to move to B.C.," Wendy recalls. "She said they'd had a family meeting, and decided I should take over the company. I felt I had no choice. There wasn't anyone else to do it." In 1991, Wendy and John agreed to move to Saskatoon, which was partway between Yorkton and Kindersley, and commute from work to home, while John continued to run the Kindersley dealership.

As if *that* wasn't challenging enough, Wendy soon discovered that the company was still in financial trouble. "When I got there and started to work, I just felt that I couldn't let this happen. I was determined to turn it around. It was a very difficult time," Wendy recalls. "We had very little production, and a lot of inventory."

Typical of the times, previous layoffs had reduced production staff, leaving a top-heavy management—many of whom had worked for Morris for years, and been promoted by her father into those positions. "Many were from the Bangor area, and were friends and family of my father's," she says.

Wendy sought professional assistance for the tough task ahead. "I asked an accountant I knew to look at the books with me." The accountant, Rob Orr, said, "Wendy, I can't see any way out of this; you'll have to let a number of people go." Wendy took a deep breath, and they developed a plan to do it.

On the designated day, they brought in a psychologist to help employees, and Wendy and Rob met with each person, offering a severance package. "We started at 8 a.m. and went through the day," Wendy remembers. "You can imagine the cloud that was over the company. I had to make a public speech to employees. It was a very difficult period for me emotionally," Wendy says. "I remember many of those people visiting my parents when I was growing up. We let 22 people go, in key positions."

Left with a bare bones structure, Wendy started to rebuild. Then the general sales manager quit. "I was very concerned about that. I was willing to deal with the financial and manufacturing sides (we still had very good people in design that were carrying the ball), but I didn't want to deal with marketing and sales."

The marketing challenge facing Morris was that, with the company in the emotional aftershock of layoffs, dealers were concerned about Morris' ability to meet new product demand. Wendy needed to bring in leadership in sales–leadership that she could trust.

Though she had no way of knowing it, Wendy's solution would change her life.

Work becomes personal

"I made a personal decision to ask my husband to come and help in that area [marketing and sales]," she says. The decision made sense. John had good sales

60   John, son Bryce, Wendy and daughter Katherine
        in 2004 at a relative's wedding.

experience. At 24, he'd taken over the Truck Centre at Turnbull Motors in Edmonton, the fourth largest Dodge truck dealership in Canada. He'd managed fleet accounts of several million dollars.

On the liability side of the equation, John didn't know much about farm equipment.

"He came in green," Wendy says. "It was very difficult for us as a couple; and a difficult adjustment for the company, because nobody believed that John would be able to do the job."

But John *did* do the job, and then some. "He really created trust," Wendy says. "He put programs and policies in place that really moved the company forward in marketing. He developed a team of district managers, dealers and distributors who trusted and respected him. His weakness was that he was probably too hands on, but he really helped the company grow during the '90s."

With marketing under control, Wendy turned her attention to research and development. "We had excellent people in R & D that came forward, and really put us back in the air drill and air cart marketplace, both domestically and internationally," she says. "We were able to bring in a lot of new technology, and improve efficiencies. On the manufacturing side, we invested in a state-of-the-art plasma torch, the newest laser cutters, robotic welders and computer controlled lathes–we really moved forward."

During this time, Morris also started to focus on international markets. "It was quite obvious that our domestic market would continue to consolidate and shrink," Wendy says. "If we were going to survive and grow, we had to make our way in international markets. John did a lot of work in that area. He, and

others, focused on the Australian market–he went there 30 times." They also started concentrated efforts in Western Europe and South America.

Back to basics

Wendy describes the growth in the '90s as "a wonderful period." Taking advantage of a new grant program for business modeling and planning from Western Economic Diversification, Wendy worked with Rob Orr on a new management strategy for Morris.

When George's declining health had made him step down from daily supervision, new "professional" management had come in to Morris –with mixed results, in Wendy's opinion. So, now, she made a decision to re-implement her father's model. "We used that model to get back in touch with the customer and the dealer organization, and to provide excellent service," she says. "We came forward with new products, and kept our ear to the ground, in terms of what consumers wanted." Ultimately, Morris developed a new product line to re-establish itself in the marketplace, and to stay competitive.

One example of this was the relationship to one of their competitors, Flexicoil. "Through our own hard work and changes in the marketplace, we saw market share growth," Wendy says. "Flexicoil was selling three to four times as much as Morris in the domestic marketplace when we took over management. We saw that change in the '90s–decreasing to two times as much, then to being equivalent."

The success of Wendy and John's efforts, and those of the entire employee team, was undeniable in rebuilding Morris Industries. But the single-minded focus on work had taken a huge toll in Wendy's

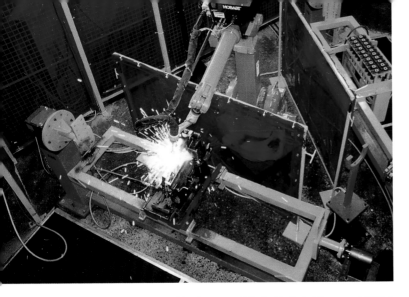

Morris was one of the first in Saskatchewan agricultural manufacturing to use robotic welding, which increased quality and efficiency. It was part of a technology upgrade implemented during Wendy's first term as president.

professional and personal life about which it is still difficult for her to speak. On the up side, she learned some tough, and important, life lessons from the experience.

"The down side was that I pushed everyone so hard, myself included, that we really started to see evidence of burn-out," she says. "It was probably most obvious with John and me–particularly with John. Our marriage started to fall apart. I had put the children first, the company second and my husband third. He was very dedicated, and made a huge contribution, but I took him for granted."

In a mutual agreement, John resigned in 2001, and the couple separated. Wendy suffered a nervous breakdown. During that time period, she negotiated with Morris' corporate counsel Casey Davis to take over the company.

"My father was a genius. He had a huge capacity and a gift to work with people," she says. "I was never able to develop the culture the way he had–he communicated that he cared more about people than the bottom line. I wasn't able to do that at the beginning because I was working for the company to just survive. But even later, when we were back into growth and development, I still wasn't putting people first. It was a huge lesson for me."

"When Casey took over, I went through a period of time where I felt like a failure," Wendy says. "Then I realized after that I was comparing myself to what my father did through the '60 and '70s. It was very different then. Adeleine and I ran Morris through its most difficult period. It probably won't have another period like that."

Wendy also realized that the reason she felt as she did could be traced back to the feeling of responsibility for family and business instilled in her at such a young age, by her father.

"The time had come for me to realize that I didn't have to be responsible for the success of the company *forever*," she says. Though she came back as president for a short while in 2005 when Casey's contract ended, her "heart wasn't in it." "I realized I still had passion for the company, but it wasn't the way it was before. Things had changed. It was time for me to move on with my life."

In 2005, the woman who had stepped up to do what had to be done, all her life, decided she could go on with her own life. She finally felt comfortable in her decision to sell her father's company.

There were international corporate suitors, but Wendy wanted her father's name retained. Eventually, a successful financial plan was reached with previous president, Casey Davis. George Morris' company was sold in June 2007, and Wendy moved on.

Morris' newest facility is the office building on Airport Drive in Saskatoon.
The company's headquarters moved from Yorkton to Saskatoon in 1994.

A father's legacy

Casey Davis pays tribute to what Wendy accomplished during her tenure. "When Wendy came in the company had to have changes made or it wasn't going to survive," he says. "Her legacy is that first and foremost, she took on what had to be done. The decisions she made kept the company going, and they were some very tough decisions, in very tough times. She put Morris in a position to grow and prosper."

Morris is healthy and growing today, and Wendy thinks her father would be pleased, too. "I'm proud of my contributions to the company. I'm not sad about it. I feel grateful for the opportunity," she says. "I have a great passion for the company, and a love for my father and my family. I'm so proud of our history, and what Father did for the company and community. His kindness and generosity, and his huge anonymous donations to charity–that was so reflective of his personality."

"The wonderful thing about the marketplace is that it has changed so much in the last couple of years," Wendy says. "The ag industry is so much more profitable now because the international grain and oilseed supplies are low, so prices are high. It really looks like it's going to be a long-term situation."

So, for Morris Industries, "It's a wonderful future. I'm satisfied that the company will carry on with the Morris name, and that Casey will continue to do a great job in the growth and development of the company."

For Wendy's part, she's decided her next challenge lies in the not-for-profit sector–a far cry from the corporate world. She's looking at establishing Saskatchewan's first "immigration access" program,

which she may also be able to set up in other provinces like Ontario and Manitoba. The program's goal will be to assist professional immigrants in meeting Canadian standards so they can practice in Canada in the professions for which they were trained. It makes a lot of practical sense, Wendy says, and it's what communities need.

Like her dad listening to farmers so he could develop tools that were needed–Wendy is ready to listen for what's needed in building this program. There's no doubt she will succeed. "My father modelled that if you wanted to do something, you just did it. So that's what I do. It doesn't occur to me that I could fail."

She's also benefiting from the many hard lessons learned in her experience at Morris. "I'm winning friends and influencing people this time," she smiles. "In this situation, I'm not the boss–I'm part of a team. And, I know that if it's supposed to happen, it will."

"For whatever reason, I never doubted that I could do the job that had to be done at Morris," she says. Part of it was, simply, that it was an opportunity to do what she does best–take responsibility. It's something Wendy Morris plans to continue doing as her new life unfolds, and something of which her father would surely approve.

Kevin & Jerry Tell
Out of the ashes

Early in the last century, a young Austrian couple from brick-laying roots immigrated to Canada in search of work and a new life. Leaving Hamburg, Germany on April 21, 1903, aboard the S.S. Adria, they arrived in Halifax Harbour on May 4, 1903. Riding the train west, they finally disembarked in Regina.

Jacob and Magdalena Tell settled on Toronto Street and raised a family, including son Adam and daughter Barbara, who had immigrated with them, and Annie, who was born three years later.

Jacob was a drayman, delivering coal with a team of horses and shoveling it down coal chutes into people's basements to fire their furnaces. To supplement his income, he also worked as a teamster for the City of Regina.

His first entrepreneurial venture was fashioning wood forms in his back yard, mixing concrete and painstakingly constructing concrete blocks one at a time. He sold them out of the back of his coal truck along with his coal deliveries. He sold the blocks to anyone who would buy them–neighbours, contractors– anyone who was building.

In 1930, Jacob made the first step in mechanizing his block-making process by purchasing a hydraulic one-block machine, and Cindercrete Products was born. The machine made chimney block, one block at a time. His grandson Jerry, remembers watching his enterprising grandfather doing this arduous work. "It was a very slow process," he recalls, "and very hard work." Needing a place to house the machine and block inventory, Jacob leased Canadian National railroad (CN) land for the first Cindercrete plant at Arcola Avenue and Atkinson Street.

Jacob's son Adam worked at Imperial Oil by day and managed the Cindercrete books at night and on weekends. It was Jacob and Adam, together, who came up with a brilliant strategy to create the innovative product that would become the foundation of their company identity.[1]

Jerry and Kevin Tell of Cindercrete represent two generations of a rare fourth-generation Saskatchewan family-owned business.

Jacob and Magdalena Tell (far left, back and front row) at a wedding in the early 1900s.

One simple idea

Like so many ingenious ideas, it was a simple one.

Cinders are ashes made from crushed "clinkers," the byproduct of burned coal. Train engineers dumped these cinders onto the ground, sometimes still red-hot, when the trains returned to the rail yard. The Tells knew that the endless piles of cinders produced by the trains were not only useless to CN, but an actual liability. The enormous piles were waste, took up space and were often dangerous.

Adam and Jacob offered to take the cinder piles off the CN yardmaster's hands, at no charge. In making that offer, they acquired free material with which to create a new kind of building block, which they called "cindercrete," a mixture of cinders and concrete.

The benefits of this product were many–being created, partially, of free material, it decreased the cost of manufacturing; and, having already been burned, the material was fireproof and had sound insulation properties. But its *main* advantage was that it made a more lightweight block, a distinct plus over building materials available at the time. All of these features made Cindercrete's blocks unique in the Saskatchewan marketplace. And, since all houses had wood-burning fireplaces at that time, there was a large, and growing, market for chimney block–especially "cindercrete" that was fireproof and lighter (making masons' lives much easier).

"Cindercrete" was an instant hit with the construction industry in Regina.

Sons and grandsons

Adam Tell and his wife, Kathleen, raised a family of three children–Irene, Bill and Jerry.

In the early 1940s, when CN moved its rail yards to Moose Jaw, Regina cinder supplies began dwindling. Jacob's grandsons, Jerry and Bill (now teenagers), made round trips to Moose Jaw with a dump truck to load and return the cinders to the plant, where they would be unloaded into bins. Shoveling the cinders was hard work–muscles ached, the boys had to be careful not to be burned, and it was an endlessly repetitive task.

When Bill went into the Navy, Jerry continued working on his own. In the mid-1940s, he remembers a particularly difficult job for which his dad, Adam, hired him and some of his high school buddies. They were to haul concrete blocks to Radville for a theatre building project. The project required between 3,000 and 4,000 blocks. The boys loaded up 60-pound blocks into a trailer that held about 600 to 700 blocks. The trip from Regina to Radville took about two hours, and they could do a trip a day. The job took a week.

"That clinker was sharp...very hard on the hands," Jerry remembers. "Not much skin left at the end."

In 1945, following the end of World War II, Bill returned from his Navy stint and set to work full time, helping his grandfather make chimney blocks.

In 1951, Adam left Imperial Oil and also came to work, full time, for Cindercrete. There were now three generations of Tell men working side by side. This was right around the time that the company took its next major step in mechanization–a step which took them to a whole new level of production capacity.

Mechanization key to future

In 1951, Adam, Kathleen, Bill and his wife Audrey all flew to Michigan to buy a brand-new Besser block machine. It was the first time any of them had ever been on a plane. The machine cost about $35,000, and Audrey remembers that transportation costs and duties doubled the investment–a lot of money in the 1950s.

The block machine was just the beginning of what was to be a much bigger investment, all of which put Cindercrete in a league that would be too costly for others to enter later.

"The block machine is like the heart in the body," Kevin Tell (Jacob's great grandson) explains. "You've got to feed it, and it feeds all the other parts of the body. The real issue is that it's very expensive to get into this business because of the immense cost of the entire operation, so we never had to worry too much, later, about competitors coming in."

The barriers to entry into concrete block making are significant–including the costs of raw material handling to get the products to the machine. It's also

Tells in 1941–Adam (back right), brothers, Bill (back left), and a young Jerry (front).

expensive to install the variety of necessary systems for racking, colouring, splitting and wrapping, curing rooms, moisture that pipes steam into the room, electrical set-ups and yard space.

Even the location made it more expensive. "In southern climates, the blocks can be made and stored outside," Kevin says. "We only needed a building because of weather. Our utility costs to heat that space for the six months of cold weather in Saskatchewan are very high.

"Today, it would cost $10 million to develop a block plant, and the machine is only $1 million of that," he says.

Once they had the block machine, the Tells also started investing in better material handling systems that reduced dust (thereby improving air quality) and equipment that made the work safer and less physically taxing on employees–like "cubing machinery." Up to

Besser block machine that advanced mechanization at Cindercrete in 1951.

that point, workers had to pull the concrete blocks off an assembly line, by hand, and stack them onto four-by-four pallets, creating the cubes. "Their hands would be bleeding stacking these cubes," Jerry says.

Even with increased mechanization, the work wasn't *easy*. But every little bit helped.

The company expanded in 1954, when Bill moved to Saskatoon with Audrey to set up and operate a block plant at 605 Avenue P South. As with other Tell wives, Kevin says, Audrey was very important to her husband in growing the business–by looking after family matters and maintaining the necessary support.

In the late 1950s, Cindercrete purchased the assets of the bankrupt Westcrete, at Retallack and South Railway, and operated from this location.

In 1958, after growing up in the family business, and with strong urging from his mother, Jerry Tell left the Royal Bank to officially join Cindercrete full time.

That same year, he married his high school sweetheart, Beryl Anderson, a local gal from Central Collegiate. They began a family that would eventually include three children–Christine, Kevin and Karen.

A year later, in 1959, an era ended when Jacob, the progenitor of the Tell line, died at age 88.

As a multi-generational family company, the value of working with familiar people is central to Cindercrete's core business strategy. In 1960, Jerry's brother in law, George Lebell, was hired to sell Cindercrete product to a different market. "Up to that point we'd focused most of our effort locally in the two bigger urban centres, Regina and Saskatoon," Jerry says. "I gave George a car, and asked him to go make personal contacts with lumber dealers around the province. We'd never done that before. Our sales with regional dealers went way up."

In 1962, Cindercrete purchased land at Victoria Avenue and Fleet Street and moved all of its Regina operations to this location.

In 1965, Cindercrete ventured into the ready-mix concrete business with the purchase of Bird Building Supplies, at South Railway and Quebec. The Tells operated from that location for a number of years, and then moved to Victoria Avenue East.

When the railroad switched from coal-fired engines to diesel-electric, through the decade of the 1950s, the source of free cinders dried up. Luckily, by then, Cindercrete's reputation for innovation, high quality and hard work was firmly established. The entire block-making industry across North America was experiencing the same thing and soon developed another method of making cinders–by mining and burning clay to create a lightweight aggregate product.

Kevin Tell reflects, "We knew we needed to embrace that technology to stay in the block business. It was definitely a defining moment."

Mined from Saskatoon and Regina, the clay was dried in fields in the mild months, then broken up using rototillers and fed into a 100-foot long by 8-foot diameter rotary kiln lined with firebrick. The natural gas kiln was heated to 2,400°F to bake the clay. Production of lightweight aggregate began at the Victoria and Fleet location in 1968.

Four generations of Tells

In 1972, when Adam Tell died at age 75, sons Jerry and Bill inherited the company. Bill had been working in Saskatoon and continued to for some years, but he didn't have his brother's passion for it. "Bill was an artist," Jerry says. "He just wasn't that interested. Saskatoon was more competitive than Regina and it was very stressful for Bill. He was looking for help with the Saskatoon office."

Health problems, including a heart attack, compounded the concerns. "Uncle Bill was lovable and talented, but he wanted out of the business," Kevin says. So, in the early 1990s, Jerry bought out Bill's half of the company, and the fourth generation Tell—Kevin—became a partner with his father.

By then, Kevin had spent nearly a decade learning the family business. In 1984, he had graduated from business at the University of Regina. He had been in his third year of engineering studies when he decided to switch to business. "I learned enough to be able to talk with engineers, which was very helpful in our business, and I learned I did not want to be one." Against the direction and wishes of his father, but with support of his mother, Kevin transferred from engineering to business administration. "It did create some strain," Kevin says. "Dad was really disappointed I wasn't going to be an engineer. But he eventually got over that."

During summers, while he was in school, Kevin worked at Cindercrete–doing every job related to the operations side of the business. He was a yardman, loader man, cuber, pre-caster, bagger, dispatcher and batch man. Jerry wanted Kevin to understand both the work and the employees, and to gain their respect. "It was harder on me than the other employees," Kevin recalls. "When your dad is the boss, the expectations on you are greater than others. No favouritism for sure!"

After his spring graduation, Kevin fully intended to spend some time working elsewhere, to develop outside expertise, before coming to work with his father–but fate intervened. Business was booming, and Jerry's two senior managers were aging. He knew someone needed to learn from them before they retired. "He offered me a position right then," Kevin says. "He said, 'You can come in now, or I have to go hire someone and you can come in later.'"

Kevin decided that, since he knew he would end up at Cindercrete, he might as well come on board immediately. "Looking back, it's probably my only misgiving that I didn't go *away* to university–because I knew I'd end up living back here. It was my only chance to get experience elsewhere."

When Kevin arrived and asked his dad what his job description was, Jerry said, "Get involved."

The first plant to be set up outside Regina was in Saskatoon in 1954.

A young future CEO, Kevin Tell, with father, Jerry, sister, Christine, mother, Beryl, and sister, Karen, in 1972.

Chain of command and generational power changeover issues can cause difficulties in the workplace–one reason many family businesses don't last as family-run beyond the first two generations.[2] "It was difficult to do things right when everyone treated me with trepidation," Kevin says. "Employees didn't know how to deal with me. If they did what I said, would it be in conflict with orders from Dad? I had responsibility, but no authority."

It was tough, but, as Jerry says, "I knew Kevin needed to learn all the office aspects of the business to be able to rise to a position of corporate leadership."

Kevin says, "At a certain point, out of frustration, I actually had to make myself general manager–and then Dad said, 'What took you so long?' It absolutely floored me. I'd been waiting for his approval and recommendations. A light bulb went on after that: *He expects me to go and make it happen.* It was a huge defining moment in my career and my relationship with him. In hindsight, I see how ingenious it was. The way he knew I was ready was when I finally stopped waiting for him and just did it."

Kevin says that's how Jerry manages–he observes people, quietly, for a long time. "Bill McMillan is a great example," Kevin says. "He was a truck driver for Trimac who delivered to the plant a lot. One day, Dad said to him, 'Bill, I've been watching you for a long time. I think you have what it takes to help lead this company.' Now Bill's the district manager in charge of sales and operations–and has been an enormous contributor to the success of Cindercrete."

Staying close to home

While Kevin was learning the business, Jerry was focused on looking for dynamic growth opportunities. "Dad recognized the Saskatoon operation needed a lift. The lift was going to come from getting into ready-mix concrete." This became a reality in 1985. Cindercrete continued to grow–purchasing the concrete block manufacturing facilities of Redi-Mix Concrete in Regina, in 1988, and the plant assets of Apex Concrete of Saskatoon, a concrete block and lightweight aggregate manufacturer, in 1989.

Since that time, Jerry and Kevin have had numerous opportunities to expand outside the province, but decided against it. "I think we declined mostly because we recognized why we *were* successful," Kevin says. "We were the biggest locally owned and operated company, of our kind, in the province."

He adds, "Neither Dad nor I wanted to travel all the time, which would've been required. Family was, and is, important to both of us, and growing a business outside your familiar area is not only very risky, but difficult to manage with constant travel. We've instead been able to continue to invest in our

Using decorative brick for commercial and personal landscaping 'saved' the concrete block business in the 1970s-80s.

existing operations, better positioning our company to respond to Saskatchewan's economic upswing." Oddly enough, some of the negative perceptions of Saskatchewan held by outside business gave Cindercrete some of their best opportunities for success. "Saskatchewan, at that time, wasn't a place outside companies wanted to come in and set up," Kevin says. "It was less desirable–we were isolated, we lacked population, and let's face it, we didn't have a very business-friendly government for a long time. It just wasn't that attractive to outside competitors."

Kevin says they learned to eke out a living in Saskatchewan without it being a "boom" province. They did it by diversifying and creating partnerships and joint ventures.

New directions and strategic partnerships

Introductions of alternative building systems like steel devastated the North American block-making industry in the 1970s and 1980s. The declining block market left manufacturers with unused capacity in their plants. Luckily, a new market for concrete blocks and products evolved through the landscaping business. Companies like Cindercrete could now use their machines to make paving stone, retaining walls and a multitude of other related products, revitalizing the block industry. So, at the beginning of a new decade, Cindercrete made yet another significant strategic, and ultimately very successful, decision.

In 1990, Cindercrete partnered with Target Products, a large family-owned company out of British Columbia, and in 1992, the Saskatoon plant began producing dry mix products, such as "shotcrete" (a spray-able "liquid concrete" used as

lining to stabilize mine walls) and supplying products and equipment to mining companies like Cameco and Cogema (now Areva). This included building a state-of-the-art concrete plant at the Cluff Lake mine. When Areva closed Cluff Lake, the plant was moved to Cameco's Rabbit Lake mine, where it continues to operate.

"We recognized we didn't have all the expertise," Kevin says. "We needed to search for those who had the knowledge. We still do. Things happen in a month in the industry that we don't experience in 10 years– simply because of the difference in volume we do compared to companies in much bigger markets. We've done that [found expertise] very successfully with the Target partnership."

Centralizing production was a key next step. In 1990, they dismantled block-making operations in Regina and moved all operations to one "superplant" in Saskatoon. The overall expense of setting up,

71

maintaining, and modernizing various systems in two places had become too high, but the family lived in Regina, so the decision to move their entire production to a city in which they didn't live was a big one.

By the 1990s, Cindercrete was diversified, well positioned, had a growing workforce (many of whom were immigrants from the Tells' native Austria, and Russia), and was engaged in strategic partnerships.

What came next was so outside anything that their forefathers had ever envisioned, that it surprised everyone: real estate development.

From concrete to real estate

"It really turned around Saskatoon and moved us up a notch when we started selling property," Kevin says.

The need for the whole Cindercrete operation in Regina to be relocated, turned the land acquired in the 1960s into a liability. And, to make matters worse, real estate projects were not looked on favourably at the time by the chartered banks. This was an aftershock of the 1992 Olympia & York bankruptcy, the largest in history to that point, which had caused a worldwide banking crisis.[3]

"We again realized we needed different expertise to stay in business," Kevin says. Setting two major goals (stabilizing financing and improving the entire employee health/welfare and profit sharing plan with management) led Cindercrete to re-hire former Saskatoon branch manager Kevin Reese as a chartered accountant in 1995. "We needed his kind of expertise in-house," Kevin Tell says. "His financial knowledge helped us find a new bank partner; develop a whole new level of accounting, cost controls, and computerization, and learn the real estate development game. It was a lot of change in a short time–but things moved positively in leaps and bounds at that point."

With their block making "superplant" in Saskatoon, Cindercrete made a few more moves. In 1992, their head office moved to its present location on Highway #1, east of Regina, and its Trans-Mix Division to 10th Avenue and Reynolds Street in Regina. They then serviced and sold about 17.4 acres of land to Price Club Canada Real Estate Inc. (now Costco).

"We were really forced into the real estate business with the relocation of our Regina operations," Kevin says. "We decided to orchestrate our departure rather than have it dictated to us."

The land left behind became a non-conforming land use. "With underground gas and oil tanks, this property had little marketability as raw land, but we embraced the development challenge," Kevin says. The high cost of reclamation meant that, as it was, Cindercrete "…couldn't give it away." By turning it into development property, they sold a portion for some $22 million. Along with the commercial Costco property development, the residential and commercial River Bend project kick-started Regina's east side commercial boom that continues today.

A family of employees

Just as when Jerry Tell watched his grandfather, Jacob, making concrete blocks from hand-made wooden forms in his back yard on Toronto Street in the 1930s–it is *family* that still anchors the identity and culture of Cindercrete. Today, though, family means more than just those with the last name of "Tell."

Generations of other families can say their fathers worked at Cindercrete. Remember George Lebell? His son, Russ, is now Cindercrete's southern Saskatchewan sales representative. He's been with the company for more than 20 years.

"When you hire family, there's a level of trust," Kevin says. "We have a distinct advantage over the big companies we compete with because of this difference. The employees are the measure of your business. We understand that, and we've tried to create a great place to work–a place where people are looked after–because we need those people to be happy and stay with us."

In the mid-1990s, Cindercrete implemented a health and welfare plan, a pension for all employees and a profit sharing plan for management.

Even with union contracts, Kevin says, as a family-owned and-run company, they still have an advantage over larger unionized environments. "As our business has grown–pretty much tripled–since I started, our work force has grown to 75 employees, depending on the season," Kevin says. "We are unionized, but we maintain that our contracts allow us a competitive advantage in our markets due to our emphasis on flexibility to allow us to serve our customers better. Also, for our management, this is a great company to work for; not just because of competitive benefits, but flexibility and freedom that bigger companies can't offer."

The Cindercrete family also includes the business relationships they've nurtured over time. "We built personal relationships with the contractors," Jerry says. "They'd come in for coffee and smokes, and take a look at the jobs we were working on. It

A modern Cindercrete plant opened in 1964 on Highway #1 just east of Regina.

developed a camaraderie they didn't always experience with other manufacturers."

One of those long time business relationships, enjoyed by Kevin now, is with the vice president of cement sales and marketing for Lehigh-Hanson Cement–one of Cindercrete's major suppliers. He is Shawn McMillan and is the son of Cindercrete's long-time employee, Bill McMillan–the man that Kevin's father kept an eye on for years before hiring him away from another firm and, eventually, promoting him to district manager for sales and operations.

Shawn says, "I've known Kevin and Jerry for 30 years, I actually used to work for them alongside Kevin in their Regina block operation in the late '70s, when we were going through university. We have had a unique relationship, as my father is part of their management team."

Being at another firm has given Shawn the ability to see Cindercrete from a distance as well, and he comments on the impact the company has had in the industry, and on the province. "Cindercrete is a long-term quality business that has been a part of the growth in Saskatchewan for many decades," he says. "The unique position that construction material suppliers have is that they can drive down the street and look at buildings they've built. These projects are vast and many are high profile within the centres of Saskatchewan. Cindercrete has played a significant role and has built [its] reputation on providing quality products and services for the construction industry."

"Owning a company in a community where we grew up and continue to live gives us the distinct advantage of knowing everyone in our industry," says Kevin. "The flexibility of decision-making also allows us to keep a step ahead of our competitors who are affected by other regional and national factors."

The company has faced many challenges over its 75-year history. There have been many periods of tough markets and lean times for various product lines. Even the "Saskaboom" of recent years has created industry down sides. "The cost of labour alone has doubled in the last five years," Kevin says.

One of Cindercrete's current challenges is, paradoxically, that they're *too* busy; and, of course, there's always the future to be concerned with. "So many questions," Kevin says. "Where are the markets going? Do we invest in higher capacity? Globalization has created a new competitiveness in our industry–companies are getting bought up all the time. One minute you've got a customer base, the next you don't. And, we're experiencing a dwindling amount of customers because of buying groups like big-box stores."

Lessons learned

So what have the Tells learned? It's a long list that includes the importance of centralization and diversification, how joint ventures can help long-term profitability and viability, to be cautious about expansion, and to stay with what (and where and who) you know.

Here's a Tell business primer:
- Buying out competitors can be a success strategy;
- Look after the business first, and it will look after its shareholders;
- Nurture your bankers (or your source of credit), especially during the good times;
- Invest in your people, they are the measure of your business, and your image–choose them wisely and treat them well;
- Having ethics and morals does have a place in business;
- Check your ego at the door each and every day;
- Have a good product line–the best you can make, and promote it properly;
- It's ok to like your assets a lot, but don't ever fall in love with them!
- And never, ever, say "always" or "never."

When called on to self-identify success traits, father and son both consider thoughtfully. "We have all had the ability to see potential in our key employees and allow them to realize it," Kevin says finally. "I think we've been willing to take calculated chances, and to see the big picture. We've had strong faith."

Jerry adds, "You have to be sold on your product so you can make a guarantee and stand behind it."

What's next?

Kevin reflects on the future–focusing on the idea that there has to be a certain amount of flexibility of thinking as times, markets and consumers continue to demand change. "Sometimes, a family business can be many businesses over time. We have continued to grow certain businesses, but there's no guarantee we'll continue to do that. Sometimes, keeping the family business *strong* means changing what it is," he says.

"Our current business is concrete and real estate– but it may not be in the future. Or it might be. We'll never actually know until we get there. And, at some point, my day will be done and I'll pass the torch, hopefully, to my family; and the sky's the limit for them."

He goes on to talk about the life span of assets. "There are times when certain assets outlive their usefulness for a family. As the managing partner, right now, I'm open to all of that because I owe it to the family and my employees to keep our family business (as I envision it) strong and thriving. It doesn't mean holding on to assets until they burn and die."

Yet another of the challenges for keeping any company strong and current.

"Thinking about what else we can do is the biggest challenge, and opportunity. World markets, changing technology–things are changing in crazy ways these days. It will be our kids' challenge to decide."

Yet, Kevin is also very respectful of what, and who, has gone before. "I don't want to make too many changes while my dad's still here. You want to act respectfully. I recognize my dad as the true entrepreneur here. He's a builder. No matter what, he's always

Kevin Tell's progeny are fifth generation descendants of Cindercrete founder, Jacob Tell. In 2007, with wife Donna, and children Nicholas (born 1998) and Madeleine (born 2000).

ready to move on to the next challenge," Kevin says. "In fact, at times, it's been *me* holding things back!"

At the end of the day, Kevin adds, if you surround yourself with good people, believe in your people and let them "do their thing"–there's no challenge that can't be met. "We have the best people," he says. "There's nothing we can't do."

Only time will tell if there is to be a fifth-generation Tell running Cindercrete, but even if that doesn't happen, Jacob Tell's legacy will have outlived most others on the list of Canadian family-owned and run businesses. From a man building bricks, one at a time, in a back yard to a thriving business in concrete and real estate–the Tells have made it through the tough times and now, as Kevin says, "The sky's the limit."

Wade Mitchell
Never say die

It was Friday, August 4, 2006–the beginning of the Civic Holiday weekend, but it would be no holiday for Wade Mitchell. The 48-year-old president of ASL Paving in Saskatoon left his office and went home. After a long week of work, Wade was grateful to put up his feet and relax. He watched a couple of movies on television, and went to bed around 11 p.m.

He didn't wake up until Monday and when he did, he found himself in Saskatoon's Royal University Hospital.

Wade's wife Karen told him she hadn't been able to wake him on Saturday morning. By noon, in a panic, she had phoned for an ambulance. Dr. Chris Voll, the neurologist who had attended to Wade when he arrived at emergency, visited soon after Wade woke. Dr. Voll told Wade that he'd been in a coma for the past three days, having suffered a bilateral brain stem stroke sometime on Friday night.

The good news was that, because this type of stroke affects both sides of the brain, it did not paralyze the young executive. He did, however, suffer from an optic condition called strabismus (one eye pointed off to the left), which required him to wear an eye patch for nearly three years.

The best news was that Wade survived at all.

But it was strange that the doctor couldn't find out what caused the stroke. None of the usual causes (detected about 90% of the time) were present. More tests were conducted and though they never did find the cause, they found something else–a potentially fatal valve anomaly called arteriovenous malformation (AVM).

"Here's the lucky part," Wade says. "They would've never found the AVM if I hadn't had the stroke."

He'd been born with a tangle of extra veins in his brain which, without treatment, would become increasingly life threatening. "The doctor told me there was about a 2-4% chance this thing would kill me–but that was cumulative, 2-4% per year! So, I did the math and decided I'd better, eventually, get the treatment."

Before he could deal with the AVM, Wade faced a painful and rigorous rehabilitation.

L to R: James Fraser, general manager of ASL Saskatoon; and ASL Paving co-owners Wade Mitchell, president, and David Paslawski, vice president.

Daughter Gillian, Wade, son Drew, wife Karen and son Evan.

Recovery the hardest job

After 11 days in Royal University Hospital, Wade was transferred to City Hospital, where he lived for the following two months. The doctors told him he would be able to regain movement and independence, but it would be extremely difficult work.

Wade couldn't walk, talk or even go to the bathroom by himself. His memory was sketchy; and he didn't understand how to read a newspaper. He had "left-side neglect," which meant he would bump into things on his left side. The therapy was grueling, and Wade was lonely. He missed his family–Karen, their 13-year-old daughter Gillian, and sons Evan, 21, and Drew, 19. They visited daily, but hospital nights were long.

Eventually he went home, but he was still taking therapy as an outpatient. It was frustrating for a man used to a high level of activity and achievement. Doing word search puzzles was part of his therapy, and he knew the daytime television schedule "like the back of my hand," he says. Four months can feel like a lifetime. That's how long his rehabilitation took.

"Many thought I wouldn't be coming back," Wade says. "I worked damned hard," he says of his rehab time. "I was bound and determined. The doctors thought I wouldn't work again, but the Scotsman in me said, 'That's not on. I'm going back.'"

One Saturday, while still in rehab, he got a day pass to have Karen bring him to ASL. It was a big day for him. "It was only one hour, but it was great. I love this place," he says. "I'd lost most of my short term memory, though, and right before I'd left, we had installed a new alarm system. When we came in the building, the alarm went off. Karen asked me for the code. Well, I'd forgotten we even installed it, much less what the code was." Security company staff arrived, and eventually sorted things out, but it reminded the Mitchells that even though Wade could remember the names of long-term staff as they walked by their offices, "I couldn't remember the new guy's name."

When they left, some of the staff were outside and greeted Wade. "It was the first time I realized I must be in tough shape. The guys were taken aback. I must've looked like a bumbling idiot."

But, amazingly, on December 15 of that year, only four and a half months after his stroke, Wade Mitchell walked back through the doors of ASL. He didn't come back full time at that point, but he was functioning and improving every day. "My batteries ran down easier and I'd have to rest," he says. "I still do. But I wasn't in a wheelchair."

Wade's dedication, not only to get healthy again, but also to actually return to work, had little to do with money. "It was much more about my love of the place, and loyalty." The loyalty instilled in him by his predecessors, most notably company co-founder, Norman E. "Ted" Greenaway, under whom he served from the time he started at ASL in 1980, until Mr. Greenaway's retirement in August 1996. "Mister Greenaway" (which everyone called him, Wade says) reminded the young accountant of his father and grandfather–in many, many ways.

Cut from the same cloth

Wade's grandfather, Charles, had homesteaded in Cardross, 100 kilometres south of Moose Jaw, in 1906. There were no trees at all, only barren, windswept prairie. The community had to make the land their own, and build everything they needed. People only survived if they worked together.

Wade's father Ken settled, built and worked a grain farm near Cardross in Southeast Saskatchewan. He and his wife, Isabelle, raised a family of five children. "My father was hard working and demanded the best of us," Wade says. Ken was also a man who believed in helping others, as his father had done before him. "He always told us, 'There will always be someone you can take care of. Go out there and find them.'"

"We learned from our dad and grandfather the rules that I still live by," Wade says. "If someone needs help–you help them. The pretenders–you tolerate them. The snake oil salesmen–you just ignore them."

Armed with those guidelines for life and a strong work ethic, Wade came to the University of Saskatchewan in 1974 to study commerce with an accounting major. He completed all but three credits by 1980. He landed accounting jobs at a water-conditioning company and a car dealership in Moose Jaw, but he knew that he didn't want to be a chartered accountant. He wanted to work in industry.

Then came the day that would change his life.

"I answered an ad for an 'accountant familiar with multiple companies,'" Wade says. It was ASL Paving. "I was hired by a great guy who left the company, and who I eventually hired back."

Wade worked his way up through all the accounting jobs, from invoicing to credit to cost accounting, and he did it all under the eagle eye of the man who had co-founded the company in 1950, Mr. Greenaway.

Mr. Greenaway and John Flood had started Asphalt Services Ltd. to service the urban paving market in Saskatchewan. They were responding to what they saw as a market opportunity–a growing need in towns and cities for street paving, parking lots and commercial developments.

By the mid-1950s, the company had established paving operations in Saskatoon, Swift Current and Red Deer. The partners acquired a small crusher in the late 1950s, and in 1960 started a new company, Star Blacktop, to focus on emerging specialties.

The 1960s were an enormous growth period, with acquisitions of Jim Patrick Sand and Gravel, of

Wade's grandfather, Charles, and father, Ken, enjoy a field meal delivered to them during harvest in the 1950s.

One of the first portable plants, the "one-man band" of the paving business.

Saskatoon, allowing ASL to have full crushing capabilities; T.J. Pounder Ltd. and North Star Transport.

The next decade was a time of strategic honing of assets. They sold some of their operations, and at the same time, expanded into new areas and subsidiary businesses. By the early '80s, the company had either dismantled or sold off all business not directly related to paving services.

In 1980, the founders joined with 10 shareholders to form ASL Paving, Ltd. In 1985, Mr. Greenaway retired, and Allan Fraser became president. In 1988, ASL bought South Construction in Regina and officially entered the Regina paving market.

In 1991, Allan Fraser retired, and John's son, David Flood, became president, and by 1992, the group of 12 shareholders was consolidated down to three: Dave Flood, Morris Hnatiw and Wayne Jorgenson.

In 1995, acquisitions continued with the purchase of Interprovincial Concrete Ltd. assets, allowing expansion into the concrete business. Wade and Dave Paslawski took over shares in March 2004, but Dave Flood stayed on as president until July 2006, when Wade became president—just a month before his fateful stroke. In December 2006, Dave Flood retired.

Though they were all good men, it was Mr. Greenaway who had the most influence on Wade.

The man they called "Mr. Greenaway"

At 6 foot, 3 inches, Norman E. "Ted" Greenaway was a large, imposing man with equally big expectations of himself—and others. Mr. Greenaway's larger-than-life persona was enhanced by a heroic story set during World War II, during his service in the Ferry Command based out of Dorval, Quebec. It was a harrowing story of survival under the worst of conditions. Like many veterans, Ted didn't often tell this story himself, but it was recorded in post-war history books.

The work of the Ferry Command was shuttling airplanes from North American factories to the European and African war theatres. It was brave work, and incredibly dangerous.

On October 14, 1943, the Hampden AE 309 bomber that Ted and his two colleagues, Robert Coffman and Ronald Snow, were transporting from Scotland to British Columbia had to crash-land in the middle of the North Atlantic between Iceland and Greenland, due to a malfunction with the port engine. Though Coffman, the pilot, did everything possible and kept the plane airborne for more than an hour, it eventually went into a tight spin and began to drop out of the sky. At 1,000 feet, Coffman managed to get the plane straightened out and they landed on water, near what they thought was the Greenland coast. Pulling out a rubber dinghy, they jumped in just as the bomber sank beneath the chilly water.

Once in the dinghy, they made their way toward the rocky shore, which took all night and most of the next morning. When they finally pulled themselves, onto the rock, they realized it wasn't the mainland at all. They were on a small rock island, still too far from the mainland coast.

They spent the next nine days rationing their meagre food and water supplies, signalling ships and planes, and massaging each other's feet to help prevent frostbite (a losing battle). Eventually, with hope wearing thin, they just tried to stay warm, talked of old times and prayed together.

Finally, a miracle happened: a Norwegian vessel, the Polar Bjorn, stopped nearby to repair engine trouble. She was the last ship of the year to come through the iceberg-strewn passage. With frostbitten fingers, the men weakly tried to use their light-reflecting heliograph and flares to signal the ship. They signalled for more than three hours before finally attracting the attention of an American army major on board. They were rescued.

As author, Joyce Hibbert, later wrote in *Fragments of War: Stories from Survivors of World War II:* "Of the three men, Ted Greenaway suffered the most serious consequences…Doctors worked diligently to save his feet while performing necessary toe amputations and skin grafting operations."[1]

Ted told Hibbert he preferred, for the most part, to "forget the Greenland incident." He stated, with matter-of-factness: "I eventually lost all of some of my toes and portions of others, but I retained the balls of my feet and my balance was unaffected. My walking has been restricted but otherwise, no ill effects."[2] Spoken like a true hero, as the injury, in

ASL's first owner, "Ted" Greenaway with an Asphalt Services Ltd. paving truck in the 1950s.

fact, caused a permanent and, no doubt, painful physical disability.

"He had to have special shoes–and had to stomp around–which just increased the sense of his meanness and toughness," Wade remembers. Picturing Mr. Greenaway makes Wade smile. "He was a lot like my dad. He expected and demanded a lot. We liked each other."

In fact, Wade recalls a meeting between his parents and Mr. Greenaway that had him tense to the point of fearing for his job. "One night, my mom and dad were in Saskatoon and I brought them in at 8 p.m. to see where I worked, and realized that Mr. Greenaway was still in his office," Wade says. "He was in his early 60s at the time. I said to my parents as we walked by his office, 'Don't disturb him.' But he heard us, and came out."

"Mitchell," Mr. Greenaway bellowed. "Introduce me!"

Wade nervously made the introductions, and waited while they were invited into the boss' office for a chat. They sat and talked "like old friends" for about 30 minutes. Suddenly, Wade's father stood up and said, "I'm done" and summarily walked out of the office.

Terrified, Wade looked for a reaction from Mr. Greenaway, but there was none. Wade continued showing his parents around the office and plant, all the while thinking he'd be looking for a new job the next day.

The next morning, Mr. Greenaway called him in to his office. "Mitchell. I liked your parents." Succinct words that were a great relief to the anxious young employee. "It was also further evidence that my father and the boss were cut from the same cloth," Wade says.

Over the years, Wade learned that under Mr. Greenaway's gruff exterior was a generous man who was protective of his employees–some might even say to a fault. "I saw the books. I know that, sometimes, he would not take pay so he could top up retirees' pensions," Wade says. "The men who use that money to buy bread today have no idea that's where that money came from."

Another measure of Mr. Greenaway was his devotion to contributing back to the company. "He was very unassuming about the wealth he had created," Wade says. "If you met him on the street, he would just look like an average Joe. Everything was about giving money back to the business."

In September 2000, Mr. Greenaway died of a stroke while visiting his family, and a leadership era of ASL Paving came to an end. But long before his end, the larger-than-life hero had instilled in one of his long-time employees a deep desire to follow in his footsteps.

Equal, but different: finding the right partner

In the early 1980s, Wade had gone to the company Christmas party, where 300 people awaited the annual speech from their President. Mr. Greenaway stepped up to the podium, cleared his throat, looked around and began. An uncomfortable public speaker, he fumbled through the obligatory message. While Mr. Greenaway was speaking, Wade looked around at the audience. Suddenly, he had an epiphany: "That man up there is buying shoes for this whole room, and their families," he thought. "Mr. Greenaway looked after people, and I realized I wanted to be in a position to do the same," Wade says. "I knew then that I wanted his job."

Some 20 years later, in 2004, Wade's dream to become part owner of ASL Paving was realized. "I had the audacity to ask the shareholders in 2002 if I could buy the company," Wade recalls. "And, in 2004, it happened."

Wade didn't want to go it entirely alone, so he asked the current president, Dave Flood, for his opinion on who might be a good fit as a partner. Flood suggested David Paslawski, a civil engineer who had worked at ASL from 1986 to 1989, and then moved to Calgary. "I knew David only casually, and it had been a lot of years," Wade says, "but I phoned him. We met and talked about it over a two-week period or so."

David moved back from Calgary with his wife and three children and came on board to become vice-president, with ongoing responsibility for the operations side of ASL offices and plants.

Current ASL owner partners, Wade Mitchell and David Paslawski.

Wade says that he deals more with the corporate finance side of the business while David handles scheduling issues, suppliers, equipment dealers and anything else related to operations and projects. He describes their differences and how they contribute to a balanced partnership: "While we are equal partners, David seems to like the outside world more. I'm more internal. I'm more focused on the staff issues, and he looks after the external relationships that are so critical for survival and success in today's business world. He's also younger and smarter than I am," Wade jokes. He describes their personalities as distinct, but complementary. "David's smoother, more polished." And, as clinically as he scans a balance sheet, Wade dissects his own strengths and weaknesses. "My imagination is low, but I can analyze a set of financial statements as good as anybody," he says. "I can think about cause and effect scenarios. But you try to get me to do something creative…I'm cooked."

Most importantly, there is one significant similarity they share: they are both entrepreneurs, and focus on the "big picture." Both David and Wade work together on long term planning and strategy for ASL.

No idiots allowed

"I think it would be tough to be my partner," Wade says in reference to his intense internal focus when it comes to dealing with the staff. "I'm not a control freak, but I've got 27 years here. I know everyone. I've been dealing with them a very long time, and it's the side of the business that's comfortable to me."

A strict rule-follower ("If you're supposed to vote, I'll vote. If you're not supposed to break that window, I won't."), Wade knows that he's pretty black and white about many things, and doesn't mince words describing them. For instance, he has respect for doing things the right way. "I'll never ask a good man to work with an idiot. We get rid of the idiots," he says bluntly. By "idiot" he means anyone caught with drugs or alcohol or, just as bad, someone who doesn't pull his or her weight. "This road between the curbs has got to be paved. If you're not doing it, I'll get someone else who will," Wade says.

The values learned from his father and Mr. Greenaway are not only present in Wade's everyday personal and professional life, they have also become part of the company's culture. Along with the straight and narrow "road between the curbs" there is also a strong sense of compassion and a desire to help people.

When he first became part owner and president, Wade did some investigation—taking the pulse of the human resources environment. "I was talking to a guy who has been around just about as long as I have, and I asked him, 'What do people see when a certain manager comes to their office? What do they think?' And he told me, 'Oh that means someone's going home.' That's not what I wanted. Certain things should

ASL employees "pay back" with great attitudes and high productivity.

come from the top, in my opinion. I'm willing to make the tough decisions. I want people to know they can call me if they've got problems, and I'll get it done."

As a result, he's had to do many unpleasant things for, what he describes as, the "betterment of the business".

"I've had to dismiss people; have had to make people responsible for their actions, like not paying a bill. I've made my enemies. But, right now, our success says we're doing the right things."

When he has to let employees go, Wade asks them to bring their spouses with them to the meeting. "I ask them both in," he says. "I explain why we've come to this point. I ask, 'Do you think you can change?' I've yet to dismiss someone who thinks they can change."

All this stems from a baseline of valuing every one of ASL's 250 employees. Wade says, "Through history, we've been blessed with good markets and bad, good aggregates and bad, but the common thread that separates the good times from the bad is the people we retain, and we work *together*. If we work together well, there's nothing we can't do."

Staying between the curbs

ASL Paving provides road building and commercial paving services to cities, towns and government agencies across Saskatchewan. It handles all aspects of commercial and industrial paving projects, from site preparation (earth work, sewers, utilities) to concrete (all curbs, sidewalks, islands) to the final paving and beyond (inspections, maintenance, repairs).

As Wade explains, there are two kinds of paving contractors–highway and urban. ASL is the latter, and there isn't any cross-over between the two. Mr. Greenaway explained it this way: "City guys run off the highways into the ditches because there's no curbs; and the highway guys come into the city and keep bumping into those damned curbs."

The work is seasonal, and not without its challenges in keeping a healthy and happy workplace. It's something Wade has thought about–a lot. "Here's how it works," he says. "It's a very seasonal business– from May to November. So employees have to make a year's living in seven months. It means that, even though we work in our own cities, we still work 12-13 hours a day, 11 days out of every 14. This takes people away from their families a lot during a condensed period of time." Then, ASL lays off 70% of its work force each November for the winter.

As an "office guy," Wade never understood why the laid-off workers didn't enjoy their winter "holiday."

"I'd never been laid-off in my life," Wade says. "So I thought, 'Hey, you're making a good living, and you get a five-month break. Why is this such a bad thing?'"

In recuperating from his stroke, Wade got a personal taste of what the front-line employees went through in the off season. "When I was home for four months, I realized why they hate it," he says. "You lose your entire sense of routine, of schedule. There's nothing worse than watching your kids go off to school and they know you're not going anywhere."

Perhaps that explains the "giddiness" that workers return with each spring. "It's an exciting rejuvenation," Wade says. "Most make a very good wage, and they're excited to come back. It feels like summer camp."

Another challenge for ASL, has been the physical strain the paving business has on front-line employees. "A lot of these men have been around for years. This business has taken its toll on many. We work in traffic, around hoists that could tip over on a person," Wade says. "You have to be respectful of the heavy equipment–if it runs over you, you are not getting up." And, of course, in earlier days, the repetitive tasks of shovelling were especially tough on the shoulders and backs of even the strongest men.

A concerted effort to improve health and safety conditions has resulted in significant improvements. Over the past 15 years, the heaviest labour of shovelling has been replaced with machines. The company bought its first skid steer in 1994, and now owns a fleet of 38.

As cheerleader for the work of the employee-driven Health and Safety Committee, Wade proudly describes the improvement in their record for lost time accidents between 2004 and 2008. "In 2004 we had 38, and last year we had none."

Now that he has many jobs, including keeping just a bit of a hand in accounting, Wade says the only "science" in his life is "keeping people between the lines."

"I talk to people for 90% of my day," he explains. "I'm very seldom by myself. I'm not an outgoing person, but my door is always open. I give advice, I talk through issues, and I really have come to enjoy people."

In fact, Wade reveals, he's actually been told he sometimes talks too much–sharing information with employees that other private companies might reserve for shareholder meetings. But he strongly believes that those who create the success need to fully understand what it means, and what's done with the profit. "I have no secrets. People here know our revenues. They know we're reinvesting so the stock-in-trade can be the best for the company it can be."

In the past four years, ASL has doubled in sales growth but, paradoxically, they have fewer employees. Wade's explanation? "We're highly productive. It's that simple."

Wade knows that treating staff well, and respectfully, fuels part of that productivity. "People who work here are honest and hard-working," he says. "They care. It isn't just a job to them. Our receptionist has been here for five years. I told her that she has accomplished three to four times our normal expectations. You have to value that so highly, because that's one staff person instead of three or four."

Wade tells a story about a competitor asking him one day, "'Don't you like to burn diesel and make dust?' I told him truthfully, 'No, I like to be successful.' He scoffed at that–but I'm not a contractor, I'm a businessman."

And success is exactly what this generation of ASL leadership and employees have achieved. "We've embarked on quite a voyage," Wade says of the past five years since he and David Paslawski purchased control. "On March 1, 2004, we were a company that was doing $36 million. Last year [2008], we did $92 million." ASL has not only boosted absolute sales, they've also increased their market share and their client retention rate.

True to the values of his forebears at ASL, and his own beliefs, Wade credits the success to the employees. "The success is from managers, supervisors, foremen and crew members," he says. "We, as owners, have taken everything we've made and invested it back, and the employees pay us back by continuing their great attitudes and high productivity."

Some of that re-investment has included expanding or upgrading branch plants, equipment and product lines in Regina and Lloydminster–an investment of more than $15 million over five years. And, in 2009, money was allocated to improving facilities for employees at the Saskatoon plant and head office. Wade says that a new high-end locker room, coffee lounge and even shower facilities have "improved the place." Keeping their people happy continues to be a high priority as Wade and his partner look into ASL's future.

There is a conscious effort underway to update ASL's image–to recruit more young people, and more women. "We need to make ourselves more attractive to young people," Wade says. "I'm no statistician or sociologist, but they're going to be the future, I think," he jokes. The total of 11 women at the company bothers Wade–for one reason only. "It means we're not an attractive industry for women to want to be part of, but we're becoming more attractive. We have to–otherwise we're closing out half of the population looking for work. We've put it out that we want everybody. We now have five women actually on crews. We installed a women's washroom," he says. "And I'm hoping the story will be different in five years."

All that focus on reinvesting in people and the company has paid off for ASL, but is the bottom line the only place to measure it?

Defining wealth

How success and wealth are defined is an interesting question to Wade.

There is no question about the phenomenal growth that has occurred during the Mitchell-Paslawski generation of leadership at ASL. This growth is due, in a large part, to the partners' determination to pump the profits back into the company and to use the company's wealth to both expand

A current-day paving project with an ASL paving crew in Saskatoon.

capacity and improve conditions for their employees. Measuring wealth in more than financial terms is the true "wealth creation philosophy" for ASL.

As far as personal wealth is concerned, Wade shrugs it off. "When things were starting to go really well, I told Karen we could afford something new in the future–a new car, or a boat, or even a bigger house. I asked her if the money would change what she wanted out of life."

His wife's response, after thinking it over for a few days, was, "No. I can't see it."

And that was that.

They continue to live in a middle-class neighbourhood in the modest 1,400 square foot house they've had for 20 years. The old-school mantra, "Spend less than you make" has always been an important survival strategy for individuals, families and companies. It's even more essential in today's recessionary environment. "I learned that from my grandfather, my father and Mr. Greenaway," Wade says. "I haven't always lived it, but it's the only way to stay in control, on any level."

Though he's now financially comfortable, Wade says he'll never spend the extra money. "I don't want to be poor," he says, "but I don't know what rich is. Nothing for me has changed. Nothing will change."

For him, it isn't about the money. It's about looking after people, and the company that treated him so well. "I went to university but that means nothing. You just treat everyone the same and take care of everybody. That's how simple it is."

Wade reflects back on what he learned from that cataclysmic event in 2006, the stroke. "I learned that I'm afraid of a lot of things, but failure isn't one of them. If you want something badly enough, whether it's to invent a new product, improve a service, or to walk again, you can do it. It only depends on how hard you're willing to work to make it happen."

Another big lesson: Other people know what they're doing. "I learned this. I thought when I went away for four months I'd come back and there would be a pile of work," Wade says, laughing. "But in my absence everybody took a chunk and they did it. And they did it very well. Not how I would've done it, maybe, but they got the right answer nonetheless." Effective delegation made better use of Wade's more limited time, and he found another great benefit: "There were some things people tried to give back to me, and I said, 'No, you do it.' It allows people to achieve–and they have all grown as a result of it."

This realization helped Wade, and everyone else, get a clearer perspective on their roles as part of the ASL team. "Not everything needed my name on it," Wade says. "It's been wonderful. Others have increased their value and their experience and skills, and they're very proud of their work. My tasks went down, so it has been a real 'win-win.'"

And "win-win" is a very good result for the president of what Saskatoon Business Magazine named the 23rd largest company in Saskatchewan in 2008. Especially since, just a few years ago, he nearly lost it all.

"Never give up. Never quit," Wade advises young and new entrepreneurs. "It doesn't matter what your dream is. For me, it was to survive that thing [the stroke], come back to this place and continue to help keep a place going that is important to many people's lives. Whatever it is for you–you can do it."

Ernie Poole
& PCL Employee-Owners
Poole's people

When Kris Hildebrand talks about the project, you hear excitement in his voice; see it in his eyes. It's the kind of excitement brought on by challenge. Kris, district manager of PCL's Saskatchewan-based operations, leans forward, gesturing broadly with his hands.

"This unique facility has pressurization chambers with airlock doors somewhat like those you find in a submarine," Kris says. "We haven't done anything like this before in the history of our company, and it's only the second building of its kind in Canada." The three-year project is the Intervac research facility, a high-tech virology lab at the Vaccine Infectious Disease Organization (VIDO) in Saskatoon.

What you don't see in this structure is as important as what you do see. The lab walls are 16 inches thick, housing such materials as rebar, pipe and conduit. Add to this the sophisticated building systems, and you get what he calls a complicated "building envelope." PCL implemented building information modeling (BIM), also known as virtual construction, to simulate the facility's design, construction, and operation. The purpose was to identify and correct any conflicts or inconsistencies, before construction started–especially important given the tight tolerances on this Level 3 containment facility. "We're building the project twice–first in a virtual world and then on site, which helps avoid a lot of unnecessary rework," Kris says. "This project makes the best use of PCL's unique construction abilities, especially in the area of formwork. We developed a housing to pump the self-consolidating concrete into the walls, from the bottom up."

Intervac is the kind of project that best represents what PCL can do–the kind of project that would gain the approval of PCL's founder, Ernest Poole.

PCL Saskatchewan District Manager, Kris Hildebrand (7th from right, front row), joins the project team on the Intervac site.

Poole's Rules

Ernie's sons, John and George, purchased the company in 1948. To help steer them in the competitive construction industry, he gave them some advice, which has since become known as Poole's Rules.[1] These informal guidelines, written on a single sheet of his personal stationery in elegant script, continue to inspire today's extended Poole "family"–PCL's 3,400 salaried employees.

"Contracting," Ernie wrote, "is an interesting and risky business and for success over long term requires strict adherence to sound basic principles, a few of which are listed below."

- Employ highest-grade men obtainable.
- Encourage integrity, loyalty and efficiencies.
- Avoid sidelines.
- Do not permit sidelines by employees.
- Be fair in all dealings with owners, architects, engineers and subcontractors.
- Keep your word as good as your bond.
- Give encouragement and show appreciation.
- Be firm, fair and friendly.
- Avoid jobs where design is not good or financing doubtful. Let your competition have these.
- Good accounting and cash-keeping are essential.
- Do not let finishing up of jobs or collecting payments lag.

Along with this one-page statement, Ernie left a legacy of careful business practices, supported by a culture of constant growth and adaptation. The story of this great Canadian entrepreneur starts at the turn of the century.

A contract with adventure

Born in Woodville Mills, P.E.I., in 1883, Ernie Poole was one of five children. He grew up apprenticing with his millwright father.

"At home, I spent as much time as possible in my father's woodworking shop and learnt there to use ordinary carpenter's tools before I was old enough to do any heavier work," Ernie said. "Later, I helped in the mills and learnt to operate all of the machines. While the mills made a moderate amount of money, I could see that work was diminishing ..."[2]

At 19, the young carpenter and a few friends hopped the rails on a 1903 "harvest excursion," joining a contingent of young men from the Maritimes and Central Canada who were leaving the gentility of the East Coast for the wild western frontier. They all had a dream–whether it was to find work, to homestead, or simply to have a grand adventure.

The crew arrived in Melita, Manitoba, where a local contractor immediately put them to work. Prairie towns were built overnight. There was no shortage of work, and skilled men were in high demand. Ernie realized that the more skills he had, the better living he would make. Returning to P.E.I. for the winter, he enrolled in a course in architecture, a move that heralded a self-motivated life of correspondence studies.

Ernie Poole penned these guidelines in 1948 to help guide his sons as they took over his construction company.

The next summer, Ernie came west again. This time, he ended up in Stoughton, a busy farming community in Southeast Saskatchewan. He found work with James Martin—a "fine old tradesman," originally from P.E.I. They built homes, barns and stores, including a hardware store that would serve as a workplace for Ernie through the next winter. He continued his studies, and planned on a career in construction.

In the spring of 1906, the two men decided to go into business, forming a contracting company called Martin and Poole. They recruited Silas and James Lamont, who had come out on the harvest excursion with Ernie, to work as carpenters. Martin soon retired and returned to the Island, leaving Ernie to continue business under his own name—E.E. Poole General Contractor.

That winter, Ernie returned to P.E.I. for the final time. In the spring of 1907, he made a permanent move west with his friend, Charlie Kennedy. After re-hiring the Lamont brothers, the four islanders created the team that would build Poole's fledgling business in Saskatchewan.

For a few years, they had success building brick schools, town halls, banks and stores throughout Saskatchewan and Manitoba. The work was fairly profitable because, as Ernie explained, "The local small contractors could not handle it, and the larger contractors in Regina did not pay it any attention."[3]

Since no construction work could be done during the winter, and since homesteading appeared to be a productive way to spend the winter, Ernie and his friends, the Lamont brothers, got land and "proved it up" by cultivating it. Ernie found land at

A "rags-to-riches" story; Canadian entrepreneur Ernie Poole started with nothing. Shown here, in the early 1900s, darning his own socks.

Lucky Lake, purchasing two South African script warrants, each of which gave him a half section to homestead rather than the normal quarter section.

It was a good investment, but extremely hard work and the living conditions were far from luxurious. "In order to get to the homestead," Ernie wrote, "we had to cross the Saskatchewan River, once making the crossing on the ferry cable when we found the ice was running and the ferry tied up.

Through building information modelling, or virtual construction, PCL was able to identify and correct inconsistencies before construction started-and avoid unnecessary rework-on the high tech Intervac lab.

"I spent three winters there in a 12 foot by 16 foot granary type shack, and did not find it irksome. While there, I continued my studies, including reinforced concrete engineering and bookkeeping systems…."[4]

After a nasty bout of severe inflammatory rheumatism [probably from getting wet and cold in the river], Ernie set up the company headquarters in Rouleau, another busy Saskatchewan town. Over the next few summers, he employed a crew of 30 carpenters.

In 1913, Ernie married Gertrude Annear and they settled in Moose Jaw. He also incorporated his company under the name of Poole Construction Company Limited.

There were a few significant projects over the next few years, but steady work was hard to come by until the summer of 1918, when Poole Construction landed a large contract for the Fort Qu'Appelle Sanitarium.

Worth about $300,000, the project provided work and improved the company's net asset position.[5]

With the end of the Great War in 1918, soldiers returned home. There was a feeling of moving ahead, of getting on with things–and that meant building.

Having moved to Regina for the Sanitarium project, the company put down roots in the city, building its own office building and millwork shop in 1919. In 1922, Ernie opened a branch office in Edmonton(where the North American Headquarters for the PCL family of companies resides today). The post-war world was rebuilding, and Poole Construction was becoming known for its work across Western Canada.

Tough times, tough men

The sudden crash of the stock market in October 1929, and the severe prairie drought of the Dirty Thirties, caused some of the toughest challenges Ernie would ever face. Even when there was no work, he tried to keep his superintendents working. "He was very strong on the idea of loyalty, and it went both ways," recalled Harry Ellenwood, a carpenter for Poole Construction. "I used to chase the fire engines. Mr. Poole gave my phone number to the fire department…I kept a half-ton truck at home with nails and plywood sheeting. I'd follow the sirens and board up the damage, and most of the time the insurance company would give us the repair job," he said.[6]

Surviving on a few contracts that were in place before the Depression, Ernie decided to move the Poole headquarters from its Saskatchewan home to Edmonton in 1932, thinking that it would help grow the business.

Meanwhile, Ernie and Gertrude were raising a family of four children–George, Ruth, Inez and John–through these turbulent times.

In 1937, John graduated in civil engineering from the University of Alberta and Ernie offered him a job. Wanting to first prove himself on his own, he respectfully declined. John worked for a year at the Edmonton Power Plant, and then joined Poole Construction.

John's brother George earned the same university degree, in 1943, after which he served in the army during World War II. During the war, John worked for a defense contractor in Montreal and, in 1945, both men returned to Edmonton to learn the family business.

Their father's sons

Ernie's right-hand man Dick Pettinger was an important teacher of both young men.

"He was a great mentor, regularly taking us around to projects when he was dealing with the superintendents," John recalled, many years later. "One Saturday, in the old office, we were discussing styles of management. Mr. Pettinger laid a piece of string on the drafting table. He began pushing from one end until it looped around and tangled up. Then he took one end and pulled it gently out of the mess

until the string was straight again. 'That goes to show that you can't push people around, but you can lead them anywhere,' he said."[7]

In 1948, John and George decided to buy the company from their father. "He was 64 by that time," John said. "People were beginning to wonder what was going to happen to the company, so they were quite happy to see the new generation, although they didn't yet know what we could do."[8]

Partnerships fuel growth

Through the '40s and '50s, the company grew quickly, due, in part, to multiple power plant projects for the Calgary Power Company. These projects marked the beginning of a relationship between Poole and the utility that would span several decades.[9] The practice of developing long-term relationships with clients became a Poole Construction trademark, making it a desirable contracting partner. The company built a reputation for being fair and budget-conscious–traits that Ernie had identified as being valuable in "Poole's Rules."

Another important partnership that contributed to the growth of Poole Construction was with the American-based Peter Kiewit Sons' Co., a large construction and mining company from Nebraska. The partnership worked on various heavy civil projects, including the South Saskatchewan River Project and portions of the Banff-Jasper highway through the Canadian Rockies. Kiewit's successful employee ownership structure particularly impressed the Pooles.

During his 55-year career, which included terms as President, CEO and Chairman, Bob Stollery helped bring employee ownership to the PCL family of companies.

93

After the Jasper Park Lodge was gutted by fire in 1952, Ernie Poole personally oversaw the eight-month reconstruction of this popular destination of royalty and film stars.

Also during this time, Bob Stollery, who was to eventually lead Poole Construction to employee ownership, joined the team.

One of the fastest and most challenging jobs undertaken by Poole Construction was the rebuilding of the world-renowned Jasper Park Lodge. Located in Jasper National Park, Alberta, it was famous for its star-studded guest list, including Bing Crosby, Marilyn Monroe, King George VI and the Queen of England.

In the fall of 1952 the main building at the Jasper Lodge was completely gutted by fire. Given its popularity, all 650 rooms were fully booked for the 1953 summer tourist season, so there was no time for schedule delays. The chief architect of the CN appealed to his friend, Ernie Poole, who promised it would be done on time, and to make sure it was, he came out of retirement to be project manager.

The eight-month project was, almost literally, a circus from the beginning. Engineer (and future president) Bob Stollery said, "You must remember–this was in the mountains. We rented enormous circus tents from Ringling Brothers in Florida. We worked around the clock–seven days a week. We had carpenters from Edmonton and Calgary; marble and granite masons from Vancouver, and stonemasons from Scotland."[10]

Ernie, as usual, came through on his promise. With "wet paint" signs everywhere, CN opened the lodge on June 15–just in time for the American Medical Association convention.

At the end of 1918, Ernie's small company had net assets of $25,660[11]. By 1956, it would be billing $30 million[12], a figure that might have been unimaginable to some, but clearly not to the visionary founder of Poole Construction. His was the quintessential "rags-to-riches" story.

In 1964, at age 80, Ernie Poole died. Though he had sold his company to sons, John and George, in 1948, he remained as chairman of its board until his death.

The next era ushered in business growth that was truly remarkable. This growth was fueled by a radical decision by the Poole brothers, a decision that helped build company stability and employee loyalty. No mean feat in the traditionally turbulent construction industry.

Extending the family

In 1969, Bob Stollery took over as president, nearly 20 years after joining the company. John and George Poole had tremendous respect for the man they chose to run Poole Construction. "The smartest thing we ever did was to hire Bob Stollery," said John Poole.[13]

It was a time of change. During the late '60s, many construction firms were consolidating, and Canadian firms were being sold to larger companies, some of them international. The Poole brothers began to seriously think about selling the company. John, George, and Bob met informally to discuss the options. Eventually, they decided that some kind of employee ownership was the way to go.

"The first concept has always been that sharing is good business," Bob said. "The Pooles had previously done this with bonuses. I believed that by totally sharing the operation, we would bring tremendous stability to our group."[14]

The six-story, $58-million College of Agriculture at the University of Saskatchewan was built between1988 and 1991.

The sale of the company was negotiated through Bob and then vice-president Hank Gillespie. There were so many versions of the offer that Bob took to numbering them. Finally, it was agreed that scheme #38B met all the criteria.

A small group, who became known as the "Original 25," agreed to purchase the company from the Pooles. Several future executive members would come out of that original group, including Ross Grieve, executive chairman of the PCL board of directors. Ross recalled the mysterious phone call and package that led him to a meeting in Edmonton where the plan was revealed. At the meeting, he found out that there was a voluntary offer to purchase shares in the company that amounted to about $8,000. "It may as well have been eight million," he said, "because I had no idea where I could get that kind of money." But Ross got the money from a friend, worked out a repayment plan, and was in. "Within a year the company bought back my $7,200 of preferred shares, so my investment turned out to be $800 for 800 shares."[15]

On June 27, 1977, the Poole brothers and Bob Stollery signed the closing documents to execute the sale of Poole Construction Limited to PCL Construction Holdings Ltd., signaling the start of employee ownership. The plan was always to broaden the scope of employee ownership, so at the end of the first year, a second offering was made, a practice which has continued every year since.

After the new PCL company had been in operation for a few years, majority shareholder and President Bob Stollery presented an offer to enable younger employees to become owners. He would sell 10% of his shares each year to not only allow this to occur, but also to provide the company a means to buy him out over time, thereby reducing the financial burden of an up-front buyout. Hundreds of today's shareholders came into ownership using these shares.

On March 1, 1979, Poole Construction Limited officially adopted its new name: PCL Construction Limited. Today, the PCL family of companies has grown to more than 20 independent operating companies; however, it remains owned by about 95% of the 3,400 salaried employees.

Saskatchewan the sun of the PCL solar system

In 2009, news came of the dismantling of the Weyburn Psychiatric Hospital in Saskatchewan, one of the most significant early projects in the development of Ernie Poole's small contracting company. Ernie had won the $3-million contract to build the hospital in the 1920s. It was larger than anything Poole Construction had built before–more than four million bricks and 1.25 million feet of rough timber were used in the building, which spanned nearly six acres. Its base was just 8 feet short of a mile.

Construction of the curvilinear concrete structure of the Saskatchewan Indian Federated College, later renamed the First Nations University of Canada, posed an exciting challenge to the project team.

95

Built during 1920-21, the nearly mile-long Weyburn Psychiatric Hospital, which stood until 2009, was one of Poole's greatest achievements in Saskatchewan.

The hospital's greatest claim to fame, other than size, was the fact that the Poole project team implemented a concrete distribution system that was considered quite advanced for its time, in addition to introducing a formal costing system to complete the work–innovations that would become a hallmark of the Poole identity.

But nearly a century later, the archaic building had outlived its usefulness. Its continued maintenance made it an albatross hanging around the necks of the Town of Weyburn and the province.

As the building was being demolished in the spring of 2009, PCL welcomed a new manager to its Saskatchewan District, Kris Hildebrand, who speaks of the continuing significance of Saskatchewan to the PCL family. "Our district has long been considered a training ground for future PCL leaders. Almost all our presidents have worked here."

There are many reasons for this, he says, but the most significant reason is that the Saskatchewan district offers a more diverse portfolio of work than other PCL operations because of the province's small population and continually competitive market.

"People are challenged by the diversity of our operations," Kris says. "Today, we're building a massive high-tech project for VIDO and the complex Mother-Baby Wing at the Regina General Hospital; tomorrow, the Boundary Dam spillway replacement, and the Co-op refinery project in Regina [the oil upgrader]."

In true prairie fashion, PCL Saskatchewan employees learn to economize at every opportunity. "In small towns and farm communities, residents learn to do more with less," Kris says. "We teach our people to do this too."

PCL Saskatchewan people also stand out for their hard work ethic. "When we transfer staff to other PCL districts, people notice," Kris says. "They comment that we have a work ethic that is second to none; that we share the lessons we've learned."

"If I was to draw a map of culture in our company," Kris says, "it would mimic our solar system. Saskatchewan is in the centre as the "warm" point. We've learned so much here. It's a necessity to learn growing up on the prairies, and it so happens that Ernie Poole started here."

PCL's newest President and CEO Paul Douglas, who served as district manager in PCL Saskatchewan from 1989 to 1990, acknowledges the impact of Saskatchewan culture on newcomers. "If you don't go [into Saskatchewan] with a PCL tattoo on, you sure come out with one. It's a brand we're proud of."

All in it together

The dictionary tells us there are many definitions of the word "family," one of which is "a group of people united by certain convictions or a common affiliation."[16] For the PCL family, the common affiliation is employee ownership.

"As owners, we're accountable to each other," Kris says. "Every project team always wants their project to be the best they've ever done, because we're all benefactors. I can't think of a better motivator."

Paul says, "Some companies are plagued by a lack of employee engagement, spurred by such issues as poor communication or a lack of leadership. People get frustrated, and end up putting in time. In the employee ownership model, if you don't like what's going on, you're expected to stand up, present solutions and make things right. It creates an extraordinary level of engagement."

It's also a system that breaks down the barriers of administrative protocol which sometimes can impede information flow. Back in 1990, Paul started up a brand new branch in Ottawa. "A couple of years into it, an assistant came in to see me and said, 'I shouldn't be coming to you directly, but I'm a shareholder, and I think you should know about something.' I was able to deal with the issues before they became serious problems and, as a result, our team continued and prospered," he says. "This demonstrates that, at every level, we are shareholders. We can make a difference; we have a right to do so and we are empowered to do so.

"The reward is more than a share in the company profits," Paul adds. "It's the pride associated with being part of something larger, of being part of a winning team."

Thinking like entrepreneurs

PCL places significant importance on outside-the-box thinking. The work of teams that "challenge the process" is regularly published through an internal QUEST bulletin system. Each year, the team or individual with the most innovative process wins a coveted Innovation Award. Judging is done by PCLers across the companies. This program serves not only to acknowledge the important work being done by entrepreneurial employees, but to solicit valuable information for the collective knowledge base.

One innovative idea was that of using hand-held digital recorders to reduce the time (and therefore cost) of one of the most onerous tasks of a contractor, that of making a hand-written "punch list" to identify remaining deficiencies before final inspection.

The idea came from the project team on the 1,100-room Health Sciences Critical Services Centre in Winnipeg, Manitoba. They recommended using the recorders to translate voice recordings into text which could be uploaded to a computer. It was a fantastic idea.

"Normally that punch list would have taken hundreds of hours to complete," Kris says, "but with the recorders, the project team could walk the site, talk with employees and subcontractors and

Construction Manager Ray Mark consults with Field Engineer Claire Rutherford on the construction challenges of the unique Intervac lab project in Saskatoon.

97

complete the punch list—all at once. This new practice saved about 60% of the time traditionally spent on these independent activities. For senior managers, this was a great improvement."

It saved time and money—both worthwhile outcomes for this innovative organization.

Cultivating the next generation

When asked what he feels his biggest job is, Paul says, "We've gone through such a rapid growth spurt over the last 10 years, what I really want to do is make sure that employees understand and embrace our culture, including the obligations and opportunities that come with employee ownership."

And, of course, for Paul that means building a culture that continues to grow their future leaders. "When I think about it, I took on senior management roles in my late 20s. I was already being groomed for bigger and better things. PCL invested in my future. It's why I stayed."

He says the situation that PCL is in (and shared by every company in North America) is the layers of Baby Boomers in senior management—opportunities for young people to move up aren't there.

"It's a ceiling we need to punch holes in, to move the younger generations through," Paul says. "It takes a conscious effort on our part, through effective succession planning, to create opportunities for our future leaders to gain the experience necessary to take over the company in the next 10 years [when the Baby Boomers retire]."

How to be entrepreneurial in a recession

Kris says that entrepreneurial spirit and leadership go well together. "To be entrepreneurial, you must show leadership. And to be a leader, you must be entrepreneurial."

Like a true entrepreneur and leader, Paul wants to take advantage of the current recessionary period to ramp up employee development. "It's the perfect opportunity to encourage employees to take as much time for career development as they can."

This "leveling off" period provides more time for educational activities, many of which are offered through PCL's in-house College of Construction, established in 1990. The PCL College supports employees in their quest for learning, whether it's through self-directed learning activities, instructor-directed learning, or some other teaching or learning activity, such as mentoring. Virtual "campuses," with local college champions, are set up in every PCL operation.

98

PCL President and CEO Paul Douglas shares founder Ernie Poole's passion for learning—a long-standing part of the company's culture.

A further testament to PCL's learning culture is the $13-million PCL Centennial Learning Centre, which opened in 2006, on the occasion of PCL's 100th anniversary. Located at the North American headquarters in Edmonton, this legacy building is in constant use, as employees engage in learning activities to achieve the individual target of 35 hours each year.

The economic downturn is also a good opportunity to teach employees survival skills, something that's tough to do in good times.

"The generation entering the workforce has seen nothing but good times," Paul says. "I think it's our role, as senior leaders, to teach them the survival skills required to succeed during tough times. If any company can do this, we can. With more than a century of operations behind us, we've learned to tackle adversity, head on."

The Intervac research facility in Saskatoon is a prime example of a sophisticated construction project that provides the opportunity to teach newcomers what is commonly referred to in the organization as "the PCL Way."

"At PCL, everyone accepts responsibility for acquiring greater knowledge and skills, and for helping others to learn. Project leaders mentor or 'bring along' newcomers, such as young engineering grads," Kris says, "allowing for a two-way exchange of learning, from which both benefit. In my view, this mentoring practice is what separates PCL from other builders. I call us the 'industry visionaries.' We're consistently cutting new swaths of territory, resetting the bar of safety or technology. Subcontractors come to me and say what we're doing on our job sites is unique."

Ernie Poole worked hard to build a reputation as a leading Canadian contractor.

In preparation for an upswing in the economy, Paul is committed to looking for more opportunities to grow PCL's footprint in Canada and the United States. "We believe that controlled, profitable growth will keep our organization vibrant."

This vision is consistent with that of PCL founder, Ernie Poole.

"Starting with construction of his first farmhouse," Paul says, "Ernie developed the confidence, and the skills, to tackle virtually any project, from hospitals and commercial buildings to bridges and power plants. Our people today have the same skills and tenacity to succeed.

"If it needs to be built, PCL can build it."

Ron Carson
Into the sweet light

Ron Carson's eyes light up when he talks about the Bakken play, the zone of sweet light crude oil commonly described as "Canada's hottest new play." Stretching from underneath the rich farmland of Ron's home region of Southeast Saskatchewan and neighbouring Southwest Manitoba all the way to Montana and North Dakota, it is, quite literally, the mother lode.

"It's the best crude you can produce," Ron says. "They kill for that stuff. It's revived [the oil industry] in Southeast Saskatchewan. We've already existed 25 years longer than we were supposed to–and with the Bakken play, there's no end in sight."

Today, thanks to new technologies like horizontal drilling, this once-quiet corner of the province is helping to meet global demand for sweet light crude oil, which at 41 degrees API[1] is about as good as it gets. It's great news for the province of Saskatchewan, and even though the provincial government knows it could see a reduction in activity with the recent [2009] plunge in the price of oil, it is still highly optimistic about future prospects.

"It clearly is an exceptional find, and there is definitely opportunity yet," said Bill Boyd, Saskatchewan's energy and resources minister, in January 2009.[2]

Others gush about the prospects as well. "This pool represents Canada's largest crude oil discovery since 1957," said Scott Saxberg, president and CEO of Crescent Point Energy Trust, in 2007. "We conservatively estimate the oil, in place, at 1.5 billion barrels, but that figure is certain to grow…"[3]

In the Western Canadian Sedimentary Basin, only Alberta's Pembina and Swan Hills fields were larger discoveries. The Hibernia offshore oilfield is far better known than Bakken, yet that discovery totals less than half as much crude–710 million barrels before production began, according to the Canada-Newfoundland and Labrador Offshore Petroleum Board–and can only be accessed seasonally. The Bakken play can be accessed year-round at low cost, with plentiful labour available locally.[4]

No wonder the president and owner of Carson Energy, a company Ron founded in 1974 to provide support services to the oil industry, is so excited. Where there's oil, there's a need for what Ron does best–laying and maintaining pipelines.

101

Ron Carson is a small-town boy who never saw a reason to leave home to make a living.

Staying home

The early life of an only child can be lonely, but it is often the catalyst for the development of creativity, industriousness, focus and for learning to do things for oneself. Such is the case with Ron Carson, who was born and raised in the small rural community of Lampman, just north of Estevan, in the province's southeastern-most corner.

While many kids grow up with a desire to leave their rural hometowns for the brighter lights of the big city, Ron was destined to find his calling in his hometown of 500 people. He worked summers, during his high school years, at the Steelman Plant owned by Dome Petroleum. The Steelman plant offered the most desirable jobs in the area. "It was big wages to get on at Steelman," Ron says. "I was good in sports, and curled with a bunch of guys who all worked there. I got to know the gas plant superintendent, Jim Hartley, that way. That's how I got introduced to Steelman." Ron's father Gillis Carson had also spent his last working years at Steelman, after having been a municipal foreman for the rural municipality for years. For two summers, Ron did everything he was asked, including hauling garbage and helping the mechanics.

When he graduated from high school, he was more than ready to get out and start earning a full-time living. "I wasn't the best student in the world," he says, "so I was more than glad to get out into the work force."

In those days, there was big money working in the oil industry–though a person had to be willing to deal with the unpredictable booms and busts that have always been part of the industry's normal business cycle. So, even though he'd had some interest in joining the RCMP, when an opportunity to join the force came up, Ron decided to stay in the oil business. That decision set him on a 50-year path to creating one of Canada's most successful companies in the oil and gas industry.

Ron worked construction at Steelman, and was then hired on as an employee of Dome Petroleum. It was there, that he learned the business of the oil and gas industry–doing everything from learning to operate compressor stations to, again, acting as a mechanic's helper.

"When I ended up there [Dome], I worked in the instrumentation department for Bruce Peterson as his helper," Ron says. "During that time, I got involved with some of the pressure and piping welders. They taught me a lot about welding."

Ron decided he wanted to be a pressure welder. To prepare, he practiced for his pressure certificate, a requirement to qualify for higher-level welding work. After six years at Dome, and armed with his credentials, he was 25 and ready to take on the world.

Partnership welded

In 1968, Ron went into a welding business partnership with Stan Fleck, another pressure welder. "He and I were both qualified welders at the time," Ron says. "I was looking to do something on my own, but didn't have any money. We were the sole owners and partners." For six years, Fleck & Carson did pressure welding of piping for various oil companies, each of them with a piping rig. In 1974, Stan decided to semi-retire and move to Chilliwack, so the two decided to sell the business.

First ditcher, in 1981, laying pipeline from Oungre to the Midale Compressor Station for Dome Petroleum at the Steelman Gas Plant.

It was good timing–that same year the provincial government introduced Bill 42, which Ron describes as them "getting tough" with oil royalties. "Business became difficult, and we sold the office and shop in Estevan, and equipment at an auction sale in Regina." Stan then gave Ron the backing to move forward.

Ron started over, this time on his own. The company was called Carson Welding and Maintenance. "I just took over from where we left off," Ron says. "I put two welding rigs and two service crews on the road, and I ran one of those rigs myself." Starting with no oil field equipment, just welding and maintenance rigs, Ron quietly began building a reputation for being honest and reliable–traits that colleagues say are much needed in the industry.

In a business much less active than it is today, there was far less competition. There were slow times, but that was, as it is today, an accepted part of the boom-bust cycle of the oil business.

Acquiring work for Imperial Oil and Dome Petroleum, Ron eventually added Producer's pipelines. Soon, Carson had a list of active clients. "We got to be known, and had regular customers. It wasn't like we were turning work down, but we were busy enough."

Early on, Ron had very little equipment and only six employees. A few years later, he was able to slowly start acquiring equipment. He saw a need for pipeline repair and ongoing maintenance work. "We inquired and found that existing clients were willing to accept us as being available for that type of work," Ron says.

Building a business was tough during "bust" times. "Every three to four years, there would be an upset," Ron says. "Then oil wells wouldn't be repaired because they didn't want to spend the money fixing them. They had a tough enough time keeping working wells busy.

"It was bad. Basically, if an oil well had a hiccup or breakdown–it was shut down. It wasn't repaired. It could be very minor, like buying a set of belts for a pump jack. It might be a $400 deal to get the well going, and they'd say, 'Nope, we won't start it till we see something improve.'"

Ron kept silently patient, ensuring he hired good employees and developing strong relationships with the producers by listening to their ideas and needs. That way, when things improved, he would be ready. "When good times started to come back, we'd be Johnny-on-the-spot," Ron says. "We were never afraid to try something, and it always worked out in the end. Basically, I think you get out of it what you put into it."

He also went the extra mile to ensure Carson had the capacity for as many jobs as possible. If he didn't have the equipment needed for a particular job, for example, he would purchase or rent it; usually choosing to purchase in order to enhance future business opportunities.

103

Typical multi-line pipeline project gathering oil to a common battery facility at a former Voyageur Petroleum Facility in Alida in the mid-1980s.

It's a small world after all

Saskatchewan's oil industry activity level was small enough at the time that it didn't attract many contractors. Carson Welding and Maintenance established a presence, and it benefited later when the industry grew. "When they started needing contractors, we were there." Again, Ron's foresight and patience paid off.

In 2002, Ron expanded into the neighbouring province of Alberta, acquiring Brothers Oil Field Services at Wainwright. All his clientele came from Calgary, and he soon realized how compact the industry was. "It's a small world in oil and gas," he says. "You visit one company and discover people you worked with 20 years ago are somewhere else. Once you're in it, people tend to know who you are."

Along the line, Carson picked up valuable business with Encana, Husky, Shell Oil, Enbridge, Dome Petroleum, Talisman, Apache, and a few others. Today, Carson services more than 220 clients in the Prairie provinces.

Back in 1980, Carson expanded into a new line of business, pipeline construction. It required a large investment in new kinds of equipment, like wheel hoes, track hoes, ditchers, side booms, graders and small bulldozers. Later, Carson purchased a "hydro-vac" truck—the first one in the Southeast Saskatchewan oil patch—to explore underground lines and cables. The company could now do pipeline locates with a process known as hydro-vacuuming. "We go down and expose the pipelines so we know how to cross them without damaging the existing pipeline."

"That was our first big turning point on the equipment side," Ron says. "It was a great asset to the company."

Their next major expansion idea was the acquisition of other services to increase efficiencies for the client, allowing Carson to bid on more parts of a job. It also reduced dependence on other companies for success on a job. Two of those acquisitions were directional boring companies, now subsidiaries of Carson. They have a wide range of equipment, allowing them to bore from two to 48-inch pipelines. They both work for Carson and do outside work for other clients.

"This way, we no longer had to rely on a lot of third-party relationships in order to service the client," Ron says. "It cut down a lot on organizing time. And, by acting as our own general contractor, we have better control. We have our own safety and quality control programs, and we like to have our people looking after that. It's critical to our operation." While Carson still uses third-party contractors occasionally, it's not nearly as often as their competition, Ron says.

Safety first

Safety is a major issue in the oil and gas industry, and it's important to Ron. He's very proud to point out that, from 2003 to 2007, Carson achieved four years and 4.4 million man-hours without a lost time accident. "This was our largest safety achievement in history and we hope to do it again, with help from our employees." Safety awards are handed out yearly to employees for their safe work throughout the year.

Building their infrastructure, steadily and safely, created a base on which the growing numbers of regional divisions could rely. "We have several divisions on the Prairies now," Ron says. "If Swift Current's going to do a job, and they need certain equipment, they can borrow it from another division. It creates great cost efficiencies and a lot of synergy from the various services."

Today, Ron says they have a "humongous" computer-based system for scheduling and maintenance of all equipment, and it's considered an example of an oil industry "best practice." Each of the company's 150 workstations (static and laptop) is connected via the Citrix enterprise software system housed on a specialized remote server in Regina. The workstations located across the three Prairie provinces, and about 190 corporate email users can connect to the web-based environment anywhere an Internet connection is present.

The company has also developed its own document processing system, which has the ability to generate regular or ad hoc reporting on a real-time basis for cost tracking on jobs, invoicing and all other accounting processes. The system, developed specially for Carson in 2006, has been in use for two years now.

The evolution of a broad range of services, coupled with their three-province geographical span has become a significant market advantage for Carson. "Lots of clients like our 'one-stop' shopping centre," Ron says.

Having expanded beyond its very identity, Carson Welding & Maintenance became Carson Energy Services Ltd. on March 1, 2009.

Remedial learning

"In the old days, pipeline failures were very common," Ron says, "and oil and salt water spills were very disastrous." To assist in clean-up, Carson started its environmental remediation division 12 years ago. Today, it has a staff of about 12 people (a manager, technicians and various equipment operators) who conduct environmental assessments, do remediation planning and perform actual field remediation work.

"We added it in because, in the oil industry today, we have a lot of environmental issues," Ron says. "There was always remediation work, and it continues today. We were in a related business doing pipeline repairs and work, so it fit us."

The division does site remediation and reclamation projects (like well abandonment and re-vegetation programs, hydrocarbon and salt water spill cleanup); air photo analysis; ground conductivity analysis; risk assessment (like environmental assessments); and Geological Information Systems mapping.

And, as luck would have it, provincial regulations are getting stricter with oil companies. A pipeline can have two leaks, but if it gets a third one, the pipeline will be shut down until the leaky pipe is replaced. As a result, companies are replacing pipe sooner. "A line leak is a huge remediation cost," Ron says. "Pipeline integrity is an important factor, so we're doing a lot of digs for TransCanada Pipelines (TCPL) and others, like Enbridge and Encana."

Pipeline integrity digs are becoming a necessary and valid process to maintain oil and gas transportation pipeline systems, so qualifying to perform these digs and assist clients with their "smart pigging,"[5] Ron says, is an "up and coming business."

It's definitely an area of growth for Carson Energy. "We're into it, but we need to be into it in a much broader way," Ron says. "It's a challenge for our company and we are working on it."

You don't win 'em all

When it booms, the oil and gas industry can be profitable. But many people just aren't cut out for the pressures and unpredictability of the boom-bust cycle. It often means a matching cycle of employee layoffs, even at the most successful companies, and Carson is no exception. Ron says the industry has been lucky, with the latest boom lasting eight to 10 years, until 2008's crisis.

"Some of us older guys in the industry–we forget, too, what it used to be like," he says. "We got a bit of an attitude adjustment last September."

In mid-2008, Carson Energy had 110 rigs drilling wells in Saskatchewan, with the 'normal' at peak times being only 50 rigs. "It attracted people," Ron says of the influx of people into the province. "But it hurt people who started up new businesses, or expanded, and spent a lot of money. The crash happened, and now there's not enough work for everyone.

"We've just gone through the longest stretch we've ever been through without a downturn," he says. "We've just been lucky. But it should have never seen the prices it hit. In July 2008, oil touched $140 a barrel, and then, in six months, it was at $40. It went down into the $30 a barrel range. It's going to be a while before it gets back to normal, but it's coming slowly and, hopefully, will gradually rebound."

Another challenge is the fact that there are smaller cash flow cycles within the typical three to four year boom-bust cycle–as often as the changing of the seasons. Extreme cold in prairie winters can keep equipment from starting, and rainy weather in other seasons can delay work due to potential damage to farmers' fields.

Spring thaw road bans usually last about six weeks every year. With soggy rural roads not capable of sustaining heavy equipment, there's not a lot for workers to do during that season, Ron says. "In our industry there are a lot of layoffs with seasonal people. We will always have road bans when spring thaw comes. Those are critical times–if you can't drive on the roads, you can't work. We can keep some busy doing repairs, but we can't have 900 people doing repairs."

Setting a pump jack at the Voyageur North field in Redvers.

A drawing showing how horizontal drilling is done in the Bakken Play. Superior to old-school vertical drilling, it provides maximum exposure to the reservoir.

Then, if the market is down, service companies like Carson experience the ripple effect. "If our clients cut their budgets to match reduced cash flows in a slow market, we have less work, there's no overtime, and seasonal people have to get chopped."

Ron says they try hard to maintain as many employees as possible during these times. In many rural communities, where Carson has division offices, it is the largest employer; and Ron is well aware of the impact on whole communities of the company's ability to keep its people employed as much of the year as possible. "We go out of our way to keep our key people," he says. "We're going to need them back, and layoffs hurt everybody. But the cost for paying people for non-chargeable hours is high. You don't win 'em all."

Mark Langefeld currently owns Wild Horse Farms, but he was formerly in the oil industry as owner of an exploration company, Williston Wildcatters Oil Corporation, and a drilling company, Longriders Rig Corporation. He dealt with Carson, and says that Carson, in fact, created uncommon stability in the industry. "Ron takes seriously his responsibility to those communities," he says. "He knows if he makes a bad business decision, it affects the families and communities."

Even good can be bad

Even success can have its down side. Saskatchewan, long used to losing people to Alberta, has recently been experiencing the opposite—an influx of people *from* Alberta—and with them, competition.

"Oil and gas pricing controls the activity in the industry," Ron explains. "Oil is okay at the moment, but natural gas is half price–they can't even hit $4. That's what's hurting Alberta now–they're gas driven." So Alberta companies, seeing the growing prosperity in Saskatchewan, are coming across the border to compete for local work with Saskatchewan companies like Carson. Even though he went to Alberta in the past, Ron distinguishes between his approach and the Alberta companies today.

"I have a lot of Alberta people saying, 'Carson, you didn't mind going to Alberta.' But I say, 'When I went to Alberta, I didn't move in and take business or people or work. I bought someone out. I bought your equipment and people–and clientele.' It's different." In his mind, the difference is paying for the privilege of gaining business, rather than just taking it.

"When I complain about bidding against 10 instead of four, it's because some are looking for cash flow to keep people busy. If you only create cash flow and no profitability, people get hurt. If you're not profiting, bankers don't like you anymore, and you go out of business."

Four decades of quiet growth

"When I started in the industry around here, the prediction was that in 25 years those wells would be done and we'd be moving on," Ron says. "But the oil industry today has been revived by technology. We used to drill vertical wells, and now we have water flooding to enhance oil recovery, and horizontal wells. It's been the lifesaver of the oil industry."

The next oil recovery innovation was the use of carbon dioxide (CO_2), and Carson was well positioned to be involved.

"We're a big player because we laid the pipeline in Canada," Ron says. "We've done all the CO_2 distribution for the oil companies themselves over the past five years." Though the supplies of CO_2 are minimal, Ron believes that clean coal burning, which is another source of CO_2, might spur it again.

Ron has kept his company at the forefront of other technological advances, such as those in safety and information systems, and believes that his company now has everything it needs to continue growing in the coming decades.

He's proud of qualifying to work for TransCanada Pipelines as a general contractor–something not too many companies can claim. "It's a big undertaking, there are a lot of hoops to go through," he says, "and we qualified. We felt good to be chosen as general contractors for TC Pipelines."

The growth of Carson has been a textbook case of slow, measured, expansion. Starting 35 years ago with two service trucks, two welding rigs and six employees, today's Carson Energy has 2,000 pieces of equipment, including some 70 excavators, 55 tractor trailer units, 300 one-ton and bigger trucks and 260 smaller trucks. With 170 active clients, 900 employees in 17 divisions and several million dollars in annual gross sales, Carson Energy has become everything Ron ever hoped it would be.

That growth and position in the industry has been recognized. In 2008, Carson ranked 37 in the Saskatchewan's Top 100 Companies selected by Saskatchewan Business Magazine, and moved up to 34 in the 2009 listing.[6]

Treating people right

"In this industry we are where we're at because we haven't taken advantage of anybody," Ron says. "We want to get paid for what we do, and we want to pay our people for what they do. If you go through life like that, there's nobody that's been mistreated.

"To maintain a reputation in my business you have to treat people the way they deserve to be treated," he continues. "You don't abuse people, and you treat them all equally–labourer, or whoever." His list of what it takes to keep good people in his industry includes: giving them a decent place to work, not running junk "like rickety trucks," and creating a respectable presence.

By treating his employees well, Ron has been rewarded with impressive long-term loyalty. Twenty-four employees have been at Carson more than 25 years, and six have been with them for more than three decades.

Mark Langefeld gives an example that goes farther than the modest Ron will go himself. "Ron has quietly stayed off the radar," Mark says. "He has a *great* relationship with his employees, because he's been able to provide stability, and he's very honest.

He works with everyone, including the producers. He steps up. He gives people extra time on their bills if they need it. Because of that, that quiet way of doing business and working with producers, I think he was able to explode in the industry."

Mark speaks from personal experience of Ron's support of others in the industry over the years. "I'm one of them, so I know," he says. "We got into trouble, and we needed help. I told him I didn't know if we could pay him. Ron stepped up, gave us some time."

He puts it in guy language. "When my ass was against the wall, Carson came through for me. He turned our company into one of the largest horizontal drillers.

"He doesn't use strong-arm tactics," Mark continues. "He has more of the traditional, quiet Saskatchewan approach. He's very people-oriented."

How a person is treated is important to Ron. "You've got to deal with complaints–you can't throw them in the trash," Ron says. "You've got to get to the root cause of it, and sometimes it's not easy. People here know if they have an issue with a manager they can come to me to resolve it."

He also says the quality of all his people, especially his managers, is very high. "I haven't done anything that anyone else can't do–especially if they have the human resources and help I've had. Our managers are good. People are our best asset, and always will be.

"We are so fortunate here," Ron says. "We have everything–the safety, quality control, equipment, vehicles, clientele, people–there's nothing that we lack…At this point, I don't know how we could go off the rails."

Ron gets a hug from former heavyweight champion, George Chuvalo, in the late '90s for sponsoring him to talk to kids in local schools about drug addiction and its affect on family life.

Ron's leadership has been recognized several times in the industry, both in terms of awards won (including 1997 Southeast Saskatchewan Oilman of the Year), and Carson's nomination as a finalist in the service sector category for the 2009 Ernst & Young Entrepreneur of the Year Awards. He has also chaired the Saskatchewan Oil & Gas Show board for the past two years, and will be chair for the June 2011 show.

Sharing wealth

Ron has also done his bit in giving back, both to his industry (in many leadership roles), and to the myriad communities where Carson employees live. "We have people living in most every community in Southeast Saskatchewan," he says. "We try to do as much as we can." Carson's sponsorship and donation focus is on "matching" employee interests and needs in their communities.

The $1-million "Ironwolf" mulches frozen topsoil for pipeline right of ways, trees and brush on Carson projects. There are only two of this size in Canada–both of which Carson owns.

Because of the emphasis on safety in the oil industry, Carson has contributed significantly to community hospitals to support emergency services. "We work in a high-risk industry, people can get hurt," he says. "We rely on all the community hospitals, and I feel it's the best place we can spend some money so everybody gets some good use out of it."

They also contribute to sports initiatives and many other regional activities and events.

Looking back, looking forward

Though lots of kids from rural Saskatchewan communities end up leaving for larger urban settings, for Ron Carson, that was never a consideration–nor was working in any other occupation. The 66-year-old reflects on his 48 years in the oil business: "I never contemplated doing anything else; even to this day. A lot of guys think I'm crazy to do it," he says, smiling. And, he's not ready to retire just yet. "A lot of people have retired at my age, but I'm not tired of it yet. It's still a challenge."

Besides, he's busy laying 500 miles of pipeline a year, and working on new projects, including a joint venture with a company in Virden, Manitoba. Carson is merging with them: they need some support, and Carson needs Manitoba employees, so it's a great fit. "We're looking forward to a bigger presence in Manitoba," he says. It's just in time, too. Carson is currently digging a new project to lay 15 miles of pipe for Manitoba Hydro at Brandon.

He's also purchased 20 acres of highway-fronted land in White City, near Regina, and has plans to build facilities, including new shops, for the relocation of three existing Carson divisions–horizontal drilling, main line pipeline construction and major facility construction.

Oddly enough, Ron doesn't ascribe his success to any ongoing planning processes, but much more to working with people, and building relationships. "It just fell into place; there was no vision or strategy," he says. "Basically, it has worked because we're accepted in the industry. To get there, we had lots of help from our clients. For example, we asked about their expectations on safety issues. And they helped us with that. We're now considered a leader in safety and quality control for contractors of our size," Ron says, "and it's because we listened, and we acted accordingly."

Ron says he would "totally" recommend young people get into this industry. "It's full of good people," he says.

Ron and his wife of 44 years, Shirley, have three sons and two daughters. Two of them work at Carson–son, Troye, is manager of safety, sales and service, and daughter, Tricia, works in the in-house safety division. Ron's eldest daughter, Tracey Smith, has also followed in her father's footsteps in the oil industry. She and her husband, Randy, started and own a junior oil producing company in Carlyle called

Spectrum Resources. They drill about 40 wells in Southeast Saskatchewan each year. Shirley, with son, Trent, and son-in-law, Roy Stinsin, run Carson Farms, a modern operation that seeds 12,500 acres yearly on 100 quarters of land. A third son, Travis, is in the engineering business in Calgary.

Ron isn't sure whether or not his progeny are interested in company ownership. "I was never around when the kids were growing up," he says. "They saw that I had to work 12 hours a day, seven days a week. Nowadays, people don't want to work that hard. Gone early in the morning, back late at night, every day."

Ron still works as hard as he ever did. He and his wife don't take holidays, and his main "relaxation" also involves businesses. He owns a fly-in fishing camp in Northern Saskatchewan at Clam Lake, and shares ownership (with three friends) of a 200-acre hunt farm near Hudson Bay (he enjoys big-game hunting). "I don't have a lot of time for relaxation, but I have a lot of family and friends that go up to the fishing camp. Sometimes, our managers take clientele to our facilities if they care to go. Up at the hunt farm, that's another story. It's always there, and I go when I can. Sometimes, I can get away for three days. It keeps me sane."

Their King Air aircraft, and a full-time corporate pilot, help Ron reduce travel time enormously, which is important with divisions located across the Prairie provinces. "I can go on the spur of the moment to our Alberta divisions in a couple of hours," Ron says, "and the aircraft takes some of our managers, as well, to management meetings, and remote areas to bid projects." Even with the help of the aircraft, Carson employees still drove 13.3 million kilometres to service clients in 2008 alone.

Into the future

Despite the possibility that his children may not be interested in owning the company, Ron is moving forward with a succession plan that will ensure the continuation of the company after he's decided to call it quits. It's an obligation he takes very seriously.

"I know everyone in the industry. And once you have that many employees, they depend on you to be here," he says. "I created this monster–I'm not leaving until someone's going to carry it on."

He has put an ownership group in place with 20% of the shares. It's a group of current managers and assistant managers at Carson, who already "run it like they own it," Ron says. They are all long-time employees, and he has all the faith in the world in their capacity to lead the future of Carson. "The human resources we have at the table…I don't think any of our competition have," he says confidently.

Though he'd never say it himself, Ron is the one who attracted, maintained and developed the amazing "human resource" that fuels Carson. He did it by sticking to his philosophy and treating all the people he works with like they are as valuable as the sweet light crude that supports his industry.

An employee welding pressure piping on a Carson job.

Wayne Lorch
A legacy of invention

It was 1919. A 10-year-old schoolboy in Spy Hill had an idea. He gathered together a 32-volt light bulb, some mirrors and other bits and ends; building a contraption that would project images from his comic books onto the white bed sheet he'd tacked to his bedroom wall. His friends were amazed.

Today, we call that contraption an overhead projector.

The boy was Karl Lorch, and his future was to be an inventor, and the father of another inventor and entrepreneur, Wayne Lorch.

Born in Kitchener, Ontario, in 1909, Karl was the son of Philip and Minnie Lorch. His mechanical intelligence seemed to be genetic, as his father, Philip, had a long history of ingenuity and vision when it came to things mechanical, even if he and *his* father didn't always see eye to eye. "He [Philip] was the black sheep of the family," says grandson Wayne, "but a great risk-taker." (Grandpa Philip and *his* father's relationship was so poor that Philip would inherit only $1 from the relatively wealthy man when he died, which Philip would promptly return.)

When he was just 12 years old, Philip Lorch left his 11 siblings at home and took a job as a cabin boy aboard a Great Lakes boat. Eventually, he took a job with the Berlin (later renamed Kitchener) Ontario Light Commission (the power company), married and began raising a family. In 1916, he left this secure post and ventured west with his family to Saskatchewan as the result of a special "harvest excursion" rate offered by the Grand Trunk Railway.[1]

In 1917, Philip and his family settled in the small hamlet of Spy Hill near the Manitoba border. The family (which included children Frieda, Beatrice and Karl) moved into the upstairs of the telephone building. Karl's mother ran the telephone switchboard from the house, and his father opened a car repair shop below. Philip also did the Spy Hill phone line repair work, was a volunteer undertaker and was on the village council for 25 years.

Relaxing in one of Performance Marine's South Bay 922 pontoon boats in front of the Pasqua Lake family cottage. L to R: Wayne, son Jeff, Kathleen and daughter Susan.

Mechanical smarts in the genes

The mechanical inventiveness Karl showed as a youngster carried on into his teen years. At age 17, in 1926, he built a clock radio, and even figured out a way to get the clock to turn the radio on and off at prescribed times. He did a patent search for $25 and found that both a U.S. and Canadian patent were available. The only obstacle was a $250 application fee, which he couldn't raise. He offered 50% ownership to the local Canadian National railroad telegraph repeater station man, who had taught him the Morse code. The man declined, and Karl's family couldn't help (his eldest schoolteacher sister only made $450 in a year), so the patent dream ended.

Not daunted for long, the young inventor (who had already taken over his father's garage business) built his first "snowplane" two years later. This time, he was successful in raising the necessary fees, and at age 21, in 1930, Karl Lorch became a bona-fide inventor with his very own patent.[2]

"Snowplane" revolutionizes winter travel

The invention of the snowplane is a wonderful illustration of the inventiveness and entrepreneurism that runs in the Lorch blood.

In the 1920s, there were practically no roads around Spy Hill. Beginning in early fall, heavy snowfall and blizzards made the few existing roads nearly impassable. Karl watched farmers coming into town, their horses plunging through the high drifts and deep snow.[3] He began dreaming: *Could there be a faster and better way of travel during the long winter months? How beneficial would that be for doctors, travelers, school inspectors, R.C.M.P. officers and those who needed to get to a hospital?*

With the help of a friend, George Thorpe, Karl made his first attempt at building a snowmobile, in 1928, using a Model T Ford as the base. It worked, and traveled smoothly as long as there was a sleigh trail to follow. This wasn't good enough for Karl, though, and he looked for ways to improve his machine.

He was interested in airplanes and, one day, as he watched a plane equipped with skis land and take off,

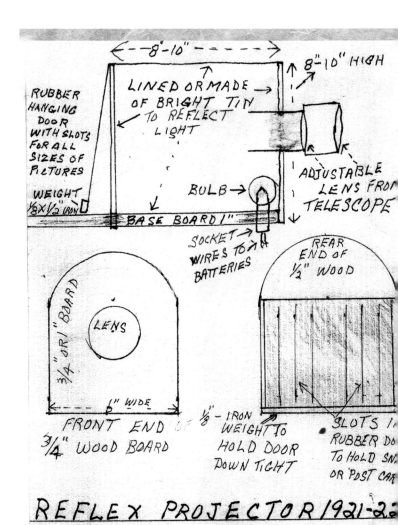

114   Karls' design sketch of a reflex projector, invented when he was about 10 years old.

an idea came to him like a bolt of lightning: *It must be possible for a machine with skis, a motor and a rear-mounted propeller to push the machine along the ground in the same way as front-mounted motors and propellers pulled planes!*

Armed with this novel idea, he engaged in many experiments, and finally the snowplane became a reality–first as a crude slow-moving machine; later as a lightweight, streamlined, swift-moving vehicle that traveled over deep snow and large drifts. He sold his first machine to Dr. Campbell of Rocanville in 1930, the same year he acquired his patent.

Snowplanes were eventually used in every Canadian province and several Northern states. They were sold to doctors, taxi drivers, liverymen, farmers, Catholic priests, pilots, telephone linemen, school teachers, hotel owners, U.S. mail carriers, the Ottertail Power Company of North Dakota and many government departments in the U.S. and Canada. The Saskatchewan government bought one, the Royal Canadian Air Force bought six and the Manitoba government bought 12 machines. There was even an inquiry from the Russian army.

At about 700 pounds, the four-passenger version (others carried up to eight passengers) got about 12-25 miles per gallon of gas, and speeds ranged from 15 to 60 miles per hour, depending on conditions. They ranged in price from $650 to $1,850.[4]

In a strange twist of fate, in 1950, a Lorch snowplane saved the life of a young farm girl with an appendicitis attack, transporting her in the middle of winter to the Melfort Hospital in time for surgery. That girl was Kathleen Mitchell who, years later, would become the wife of Karl's son, Wayne.

Karl and Laura's wedding in 1939, with flower girl, Fay Sims.

Wayne's world

Karl married Laura Sales at the height of his "snowplane career" in 1939. On the day of his nuptials, friends told him they were certain he was so hard at work in the garage that he would miss his own wedding. Karl, happily, proved them wrong. One year later, in 1940, the couple was blessed with a son, Philip Wayne.

From the tender age of six, Wayne happily remembers spending time with his grandfather Philip and his father Karl doing things most exciting to a young boy. "We'd go to grandpa's little farm for the day," he says. "Shoot gophers, eat beans, grease wagon wheels…"

Mostly, Wayne remembers watching his grandpa climb high up on poles or towers to install 32-volt wind chargers, or his Grandpa and dad hand-drilling through wooden two by fours to install porcelain knob-and-tube systems for 32-volt electricity in many farm homes, long before SaskPower got to the Spy Hill area (around 1952).

Ten Years of Successful Progress 1938-1939 Improved

LORCH'S Snowplane

A PATENTED PRODUCT

Designed to Speed-Up

Winter Transportation

- for -

Doctors, Commercial Travelers, Livery Men, Mounted Police, Mail Carriers, Etc.

A company brochure for the Lorch snowplane, advertising the new 1938-39 models.

But the real learning happened in his family's car repair shop. "If I wasn't playing hockey or baseball I was tinkering in the shop with Dad and Grandfather," he says. Young Wayne learned as much as he could–how to build a snowplane; how to properly use an electric drill without breaking the bit, and how to use a hack saw without breaking the blade. He even learned acetylene welding, considered an art by his father. "Dad taught me how to use tools," he says. "He had an aircraft welding certificate from Winnipeg, he was an expert welder. He taught me all that."

At age 10, Wayne and his father built a rotary lawn mower using a gas washing machine engine with a v-belt drive and razor-sharp farm mower sickle blades attached at each end of the main blade. "I mowed yards all around town," he says. "It worked fabulously. We sure should have patented *that* concept!" It would be many more years before rotary mowers became standard household items.

His dad sold Ford tractors and farm machinery, so another job Wayne had, after school and in summers, was putting together new farm machinery–cultivators, mowers, hay rakes, and bailers. He did all kinds of odd jobs for a few extra bucks. "Dad was also the Imperial Oil bulk agent so, before we got a new tanker truck, I often delivered 45-gallon drums to farmers in an old Ford half-ton. I was too young to have a license to drive, and I was a pretty small kid–those drums were a huge challenge, but I managed."

The young mechanic, unfortunately, wasn't as interested in school. His grade 10 yearbook, in 1956, put it succinctly, affectionately using his nickname: "Monkey is one of our quiet boys. He dislikes school and is very fond of mechanics. He has a ready smile for everyone and his favourite saying is 'Holy Cow.'"[5]

"As a teenager, cars and mechanical stuff were of much greater interest to me than school," Wayne says. "I made a bit of money, to spend or save, by working at the garage for 25 cents an hour. I set up a little shop in the basement of our home to rebuild car engine fuel pumps. I think I made about $1 per pump, which was pretty good back then."

At 14, Wayne built a hydroplane boat. "It was a real speedster and a pile of fun for years," he says. He and his friends also used "built-by-Wayne" water skis

116

and a hydroslide (a board attached with rope to the boat). All this building was to foster an interest in boats that would lead to an entrepreneurial venture, Performance Marine, many years later.

At 16, Wayne was, finally, able to legally drive–though he'd been doing so since he was 10. By that time, the roads had been raised to minimize snowdrifts and rotary snowplows made winter travel by car much easier. Snowplanes were no longer required. Wayne's father stopped making snowplanes in 1955, having made and sold 417 machines, including the largest and most powerful one-of-a-kind machine, which he kept for himself. He had sold them all at just a little more than cost. For Karl, the snowplane had been a mission–not a business.

One of the last snowplanes has been given a place of historical honour. Wayne donated it to the Western Development Museum in Moose Jaw, where it continues to intrigue visitors.

From planes to automobiles

With snowplanes no longer in production, Wayne and his dad focused their energies on the Ford dealership. Cars had become a large part of Wayne's life, and his entrepreneurial spirit started to stir. "I'm afraid that in my high school years I spent too much time during school hours designing car bodies and dreaming about growing my dad's small dealership," he says.

Wayne's dad, Karl, with his invention, the snowplane, in 1980.

The market for new cars exploded, in 1957, as potash mining at Esterhazy[6] brought in a new group of car-buying potash miners who arrived "big time," according to Wayne. The Lorch dealership had always been too small to carry a wide selection of inventory, so they hit on the idea of creating an arrangement with one of Ford's largest dealers, Dominion Motors in Winnipeg. They would sell a local buyer a car from Dominion's stock and on Friday, after school, Wayne would jump on the train with cash and a dealer's license plate. He'd drive the car back from Winnipeg on the weekend to deliver to the buyer on Monday.

During this time, television was just coming to Saskatchewan, and Wayne also became the family business' t.v. antenna installer around Spy Hill and neighboring villages and farms. "I recall putting a roof rack on a near-new 1958 Edsel with the back seat taken out for carrying t.v.'s," Wayne says. "It was interesting–in some cases I was installing t.v. antennas on former wind charger towers my grandfather had installed many years before. Neither one of us was afraid of heights."

A young Wayne with his father's employee, Ray Solway, and one of the snowplanes, a Franklin 75 hp self-starter.

117

Exciting times for any male teenager–cars, girls and dreams! "The only down side was all the time I had to still spend at school," he says.

Finally, he was relieved of school by graduating from grade 12 in 1958, and immediately looked to his father's car business, but his eagerness to expand their little dealership wasn't shared by Karl.

Lacking other immediate options, Wayne did the most unlikely thing–he returned to school. But, this time, it was to The Saskatchewan Technical Institute (STI) in Moose Jaw. Unlike "boring" high school subjects, the technical courses at STI were right up his alley. He graduated in electrical engineering technology in the spring of 1963, and immediately began working with SaskPower in Regina.

Working for the Crown

After a year, a new position was created to establish an industrial customer metering test program. "It sounded challenging," Wayne says. "I got the job and started from scratch." The mechanic/inventor in him rose again–no test unit was available on the market, so he built a portable three-phase test unit the size of a wooden suitcase and took it on the road in the trunk of his car.

He began by testing three-phase meters on electrified oil well-pumping units. To his great surprise, and to others at SaskPower, he started finding many lightning-damaged or incorrectly wired metering units. SaskPower was losing a lot of revenue. A year later, Wayne's completed report indicated that the corrections to faulty metering had increased the utility's revenue by about $3 million per year.

Ever restless for new challenges, and missing the satisfaction of sales, Wayne jumped at yet another new position at SaskPower–this time promoting and selling the electrification of oil well pumps. Until then, gas or diesel drive units powered many oil wells, water injection and pipeline pumps.

Electricity was more reliable, cheaper and cleaner, and Wayne found himself an avid advocate, selling what he believed in. "I loved it. I went to the office at night to make as much happen as possible. Dealing with oil exploration companies was great. I was allowed to do deals and make decisions with no management interference."

At the first Calgary Petroleum Show, Wayne recalls trying to convince companies with still unelectrified oil wells in Saskatchewan to convert to electric.

Karl and his two sisters in 1917 when they moved to Spy Hill. Three years later at age 10, he would invent the reflex projector.

He got creative, devising a slogan–*Pump Better Electrically*–that was applied to promotional give-away items from "penny matches" (matchbooks), to pens and even pocketknives. Companies were impressed. "They'd say, 'How come your sales and promo activities are as good or better than a private company's, and SPC is a Crown corporation?' They liked it, and so did I," Wayne says.

By 1974, SaskPower "…wasn't the same challenging and fun place it had been," so Wayne eagerly accepted another new position–this time with Saskatchewan's Department of Industry & Commerce. The new challenge was to work with Saskatchewan's burgeoning high-tech sector. "This was a whole new world for me," he says, "getting to know the high-tech companies and trying to help them grow and sell their products. Initially, they were suspicious that I was just another bureaucrat, but I wasn't. We developed great relationships. I wasn't selling my *own* stuff, but it was a close second and it felt good."

Within a year, the government created a new trade and economic development position located in the office of the Saskatchewan Agent General in London, England, covering the United Kingdom and Europe. Nobody in the Regina office was interested, but Wayne said he'd go. So, the entire family (wife Kathleen, daughter Susan and son Jeffrey) moved to London for the next two years.

Frustration sets in

"What a fabulous experience and opportunity to meet senior international business and government people," Wayne says. "The only frustrating thing was convincing the Regina staff to take seriously what I thought were *great* economic development opportunities." As a government employee, the entrepreneurial Wayne couldn't pursue any personal opportunities, and he watched helplessly as the bureaucracy back home did very little to capitalize on the opportunities he presented.

One such opportunity was an Italian technology for producing concrete paving stones. "They said installation would be too labour intensive," Wayne says. "Today, 33 years later, North Americans use them everywhere." Another was an ingenious automatic garbage container pick-up system from Germany. Again the response was, "Too expensive." Wayne notes that this technology is now commonplace in municipalities across North America.

Many other opportunities like quick-connect/locking construction scaffolding systems, accurate and efficient agricultural sprayer technology, hydraulic cylinder technology and power take-off drive systems, and clay floor and roof tiles (using Saskatchewan clay) were all discarded. Now, most of these technologies and ideas are in common use across North America. "All of these opportunities were left to collect dust," Wayne says.

When Wayne served as assistant deputy minister of economic development and trade for the province of Saskatchewan, he soon found himself criticized for being "too entrepreneurial". "My annual evaluation criticized me for running my branches too much like private consulting companies and for being under budget," Wayne says. "I thought that was my job!"

Eventually, out of frustration with the restrictions inherent in the public sector, Wayne left and started his own firm, P.W. Lorch & Associates Ltd.

(PWL) in 1984. The company focused on providing international trade and investment services. The office was in the dining room of his home. One of his early deals was a $9-million agricultural procurement project for the government of Tanzania. Finally, after 20 years, Wayne was back making his own decisions for his own profit or loss. Those 20 years hadn't been wasted, though, since they provided valuable experience and business contacts.

Many business people began calling Wayne for advice in dealing with government programs. "I gave what help I could–for free. I kept forgetting I was no longer being paid by the government," he jokes. "I did a complete review of investment opportunities in Saskatchewan for Industry & Commerce, that year. I think it was a first for Saskatchewan. I also held one-on-one meetings with business people who wanted to grow their businesses and needed capital. To my knowledge, it has never been done since."

Seeing the huge potential in immigrant enterprise, Wayne began offering immigration entrepreneur consulting services and in 1987 created Saskatchewan's first immigrant investor program fund, SaskInvest Capital Corporation.

Don't get mad, get busy

In 1989, disaster struck when the provincial government, copying Wayne's model, created a new Crown corporation to, essentially, compete head to head with his company and others who had followed him into the business. Called the Saskatchewan Government Growth Fund (SGGF), the government used public funds to set up the Crown corporation, and then gave a lucrative sales and marketing contract, without

tendering, to a Manitoba company–a move that immediately became an issue with Saskatchewan companies who weren't given the opportunity to bid on the contract.

The entrepreneur who had used $60,000 of his own savings on the first-offering memorandum, and spent years setting up his company, was *furious*. He marched to Ottawa and made a personal presentation to a standing committee on immigration investment programs. He was strongly opposed to immigrant investor funds like SGGF offered by the provincial government, but it proceeded anyway.

Then, the "icing on the cake": The government went on to sell SGGF funds as provincial bonds, which Wayne maintains, they were not. "This insane action only motivated me to work all the harder," he says.

With adrenalin-fueled energy, Wayne went, on his own dime, to Hong Kong, Taiwan, South Korea, the Philippines, the People's Republic of China, and the United Kingdom to set up agents. He sold and operated 11 funds from his home, with his son and nephew, in a one-room office.

By 1996, PWL had raised, invested and managed more than $65 million–creating and maintaining more than 1,000 jobs in Saskatchewan. "All this with *no* expense to Saskatchewan taxpayers," Wayne emphasizes.

120   Wayne at a 1991 Taipei, Taiwan, investment trade show. During this time, his company was in the midst of bringing in $70 million of foreign investment to Saskatchewan.

The federal government shut down the provincial program in 1996, except in Quebec. PWL's agents in Asia ("…who may have influenced this decision," Wayne says), continued to source immigrant investors, but all the money went to Quebec. A story still to be told, Wayne says.

The provincial government transferred management of its SGGF funds, some $150 million, to Saskatchewan's Crown Capital Partners (CCP), again not tendered. "All this was done behind closed doors," Wayne says. "To this day, Saskatchewan taxpayers are still paying the expenses of SGGF's board of directors and likely other expenses like legal fees. A *big* story yet to be told."

"… messin' about in boats."[7]

In 1997, at 57, Wayne returned to his childhood love of boats, establishing a new family business, Performance Marine, in Regina. With the motto *We Sell Fun!* the retail business sells family pleasure boats. Wayne is president, his son Jeff is general manager and daughter Susan is office manager.

As he has done in most other aspects of his life, Wayne made the venture a success. By February 2009, the company had sold more than 1,300 new boats in Saskatchewan and won Chamber of Commerce and Better Business Bureau awards for Customer Satisfaction[8] and Ethics & Integrity in Business.[9]

While building Performance Marine, Wayne has kept a hand in other ventures, including starting Saskatchewan's first Capital Pool Corporation with 12 founding shareholders who all, as he says, "put their money where their mouths were." Unfortunately, it was not successful–still *another* story to be told.

Wayne and Kathleen in Hong Kong in 1990 on another investment trip.

Wayne has also invested in oil exploration, undeveloped Saskatchewan waterfront property and undeveloped land bordering the City of Regina. Today, he manages the development of these properties.

Also, returning to his childhood love of cars and mechanics, he has built a small 1950s and 1960s classic car collection and museum, featuring his showpiece–a pink and white, 1955, glass-top Ford Crown Victoria.

Wayne's favourite of his collection of restored classic cars—a 1955 Ford Crown Victoria.

Wayne and wife Kathleen (a longtime fan of the "King") have also created an impressive and popular Elvis Presley museum and fan club on the Performance Marine property, which includes a full-scale version of Elvis' childhood home in Tupelo, Mississippi. Kathleen is in charge of the museum, which she often lends to groups who want to entertain.

All the proceeds raised from the museum are donated to charitable causes by Kathleen's Elvis club. Currently, they've contributed thousands of dollars to help pay expenses for a local young girl who is facing eye surgery.

The Lorchs also maintain strong ties to their community. They are involved in numerous organizations directly and also through their businesses. They act on boards and as corporate sponsors for a variety of activities, including the Regina Rotary Club (of which Wayne is past-president and a multiple Paul Harris Fellow), the Nature Conservancy of Canada, Ducks Unlimited, the Canadian Progress Club, the MacKenzie Art Gallery, and many others. Wayne was a founding committee member of the successful Western Canada Farm Progress Show and a founding director of STEP (the Saskatchewan Trade and Export Partnership). Performance Marine is a platinum sponsor of the annual Regina Dragon Boat festival, a donor for the Hospitals of Regina Mother-Baby Care Project and is an annual supporter and sponsor of the Canadian Progress Club's annual charity auction and the Plywood Cup, to name a few.

Legacy of innovation

The Lorch inventiveness and entrepreneurial spirit was passed down from Philip to Karl to Wayne, and it continues in his hopes and dreams for his family, Performance Marine and several other projects yet to come. "Jeff and Susan are doing a great job running the company," Wayne says. "They have a strong sense of the importance of customer service, integrity and especially community service–all of which are a continuation of the early days of doing business in Spy Hill nearly a century ago."

Wayne's car museum shares a building with his wife's equally-popular Elvis Presley museum.

The Spy Hill garage was the hub of Wayne's young life, working with his father, the inventor of the Lorch snowplane.

When considering lessons learned, Wayne stands with one of Canada's most prominent and successful entrepreneurs, Jimmy Pattison. "He said, 'Failure in life is not the mistakes you make when you try things; failure in life is when you don't try.'"

Wayne also believes that entrepreneurism must be based on passion. "Follow your heart," he advises young people. "Don't stay in it if it's not fun. Entrepreneurship has got to be challenging." Wayne points to his 15-year-old granddaughter, Alyssa, as an example. "She's a great artist already," he says. "Woodworking, automotive–that's what she loves. I wouldn't try to direct her into something she might not love to do."

The skills development needs to happen in school, but for Wayne, it was also the influences that began long before that. "I had total exposure to my dad and grandfather's place of work. I had it in spades. I *lived* it. We lived right across the street from the garage."

And the future?

"I've had a lot of fun. I'm 69 now, and I still have a lot on the go," Wayne says. "I can't seem to stop looking at opportunities from an entrepreneurial point of view. Maybe I'll stop when I get *really* old. I'll never retire, because I'd be too bored.

"So many people left Saskatchewan because they either couldn't see, or couldn't pursue opportunity," Wayne says. "But now everyone sees what we always saw–you can have a successful business here. It's not going to be handed to you–you've got to work hard. But we've got good people, good customers, and lots of opportunities. And there's lots of innovation in this province."

He should know.

As the son of the inventor of the snowplane, clock radio and overhead projector, Wayne Lorch knows innovation when he sees it.

George Reddekopp
Let's make a deal

In 1966, when George Reddekopp was 12 years old, his mom and dad decided to buy a new car. It was a major family event, as they needed to take the train to Ontario, pick the car up and drive it back to their farm near Hague. There was one hitch—George's dad John would need to hire someone to run the farm during the family's absence.

While John pondered who he might employ, his young son offered a novel solution. "Why don't I stay home and run things?" the enterprising pre-teen suggested.

His father looked at him curiously.

"I'll make you a deal," George said confidently. "How about you pay me the hired hand's wages, and give me the value of the train ticket as a bonus? You'll save all the extra trip expenses for me, like hotel and meals. And you don't have to find someone else and show them the ropes. We all win. Right?"

Indeed, the young entrepreneur had devised a viable solution. Seeing no reason not to, George's dad accepted the offer, trusting in his son's ability and unusual maturity for his age.

George stayed home alone for two weeks, milking eight cows, looking after 30 hogs, working 200 acres of summer fallow, cooking his own meals and driving wherever he needed to go.

When his family returned in the new car, everything was in order at home. George was exhausted, but stood tall to greet them.

His father looked around. "I knew you'd do a good job, and you have," his father said. Impressed and proud, he handed over George's well-deserved pay (plus his bonus), and the young George demonstrated his early understanding of successful deal-making by presenting "win-win" proposals.

Among George Reddekopp's passions are the art of negotiation, motorcycles, travel and cheerleading for his Grandwest employee team.

Elementary entrepreneurs

The future owner of Grandwest Enterprises, Canada's largest automotive accessories distributor, actually started his entrepreneurial activities long before the age of 12. At age seven, George was at a neighbour's auction sale and recognized a great opportunity. "In those days paint thinner came in 45-gallon drums," George recalls. "You needed a container to keep it in, so lots of people used gallon wine jugs. The hardware store would pay 10 cents for a wine jug. At the auction sale, I noticed that they had 12 of these wine jugs and some other pieces. I bought the lot for 25 cents. I sold a pottery crock for $5, and then sold the rest to the hardware store." George grossed $6.20. After his investment of 25 cents, he netted $5.95, or 95% profit—a pretty good return for a seven-year-old.

"As youngsters of eight or so, we collected bottles at auction sales and got a two-cent refund for each of them," George says. "My dad had a farm that was 100 miles away from where we lived. So, when we'd bring equipment back, my younger brother, Carl, and I would go along. The tractor could only go about 15 miles per hour. Someone would drive the grain truck following the equipment. We'd pick bottles, and then catch up to the tractor. By the time we got home, we'd have five or six gunny sacks full. We took that money and put it in the bank."

In high school, George was buying and selling motorcycles. "I bought my first one when I was 14 and my last one about a month ago," he says. "I've probably had 30 in my lifetime. I love them."

Guys in school got to know that George knew about bikes, and he had developed a bit of a reputation for negotiating. Friends who wanted to buy bikes would ask George for his help, and he soon began asking for a "commission"—if not cash, then something else of value. In one case, George negotiated extras into a bike deal—a helmet and leather jacket, and asked his "client" if he could keep the jacket for his commission. "It was great—I had a leather jacket in high school," he says.

George would even go without to make money. On the annual school unit sports day, George and Carl were always involved in multiple track and field events. "My dad was always very excited about that day," George says. "He'd give us 50 cents for lunch money. You could get a hot dog and pop for 35 cents, which left 15 cents for spending money."

There were cash prizes for winning—25 cents for being first in a race. The boys would come home with $2. Incredulous, their father would ask the boys how they did it. "We'd each win three or four 'firsts,' and then, so we didn't have to spend the 50 cents Dad had given us, we'd just eat leftovers from friends, and not buy any actual lunch for ourselves. It was our

126 Annie, George, Carl, and John at Christmas, in 1958.

competitiveness–what could be better? There was a ribbon for winning, and a prize of money! Dad was very proud of our progressiveness."

To figure out how to constantly progress was "in our circumstances," George says. "Maybe it was our training, maybe it was born into us. It certainly was in me."

Hard times breed hard work

Those "circumstances" reached back five generations. George's ancestors were German Mennonites who came to Canada in 1875 from Ukraine. Catherine the Great had invited German Mennonites, by decree, to come farm in Russia and, because they were experienced farmers, they became very successful. Sadly, the situation reversed for the new residents quickly when poor locals turned to violence a few decades later–destroying anything that represented the "establishment" in the infamous Bolshevik Revolution. The Bolsheviks persecuted the Mennonite farmers with a vengeance.

"I have a step-grandmother, now deceased, who remembered leaving in 1923, after the Revolution," George says. "They were fleeing down a road heavily trafficked in one direction...out of the country. She saw a chest of drawers thrown in a ditch at one point," he says, "and a little farther down the road, a trunk. Then, she saw an old lady sitting in a wagon. She'd passed away, and her family had to leave her there. That's the sight she left her country with."

John Reddekopp (George's father), born on a farm near Hague in 1915, grew up during the Dirty Thirties. Seeking a living at age 20, he left home wearing only overalls, a shirt and shoes and carrying a German biscuit and sausage sandwich. His ensemble

The three brothers (Bill, George and Carl) were speechless when they found a pony in the farm shop, which served as a make-shift home, on Christmas morning in 1962.

did not include socks or underwear. He traveled by freight train, sleeping in boxcars and hopping off at farms to see if there was paying work.

"When you grow up like that," George says, "it has a tendency to make you want to conserve and be thrifty."

Over the next few years, the hard-working farmer had earned enough money to begin establishing a farm near Hague. He later also bought the family farm that his grandparents and parents had homesteaded. He became prosperous, and was considered a "well-to-do" farmer, George says. He finally got married at age 37, to 19-year-old Annie Friesen, also from Hague. The couple had six children, including George, the oldest, born in 1954.

Though John was outgoing and verbal and Annie more reserved, the couple had similar beliefs regarding the value of money, hard work and integrity. "They were kind, considerate and hard-working," George says. "A firm grip on the arm or quiet word from my mom was enough for us to behave. She raised six children, and had an amazing work ethic."

Negotiating bike deals for kids in high school led to a life-time passion for motorcycles and cars.

George's dad was the sociable one that everyone in the family came to. "We had an extended family of aunts and uncles," George says, "and I probably have 80 first cousins. Most lived nearby; the farthest away was Saskatoon. A lot of my cousins almost considered my dad like their dad–they'd come and see him if they had a problem."

George describes himself as a blend of both of his parents, and the many examples they set would light the path of his entrepreneurial success. "We learned how to be organized and save our money," George says. "I didn't think there was any other way."

For example, choosing to conserve, the Reddekopps lived in a machine shed on the farm for five years. "It wasn't because they couldn't afford a house–they could," George says of his parents. "They started a new farm on a bare piece of farmland and developed their own buildings. Because a house

wasn't productive, their strategy was to build the barn and the shop first." The plan was to live in the work-shop the first winter and then build a house, but they ended up living there for five years. "My dad bought a couch for a dollar, took it apart, and made bunk beds out of the back and seats, putting the frame together with two by fours. My brother and I slept on that for five years. We were very happy with it. We didn't know any different."

When John and Annie did finally build a house, they built a "nice one for the day," and they paid cash. The couple was uncomfortable financing anything without a business reason, and they instilled early on in their kids the value of "not spending what you didn't have."

"When you don't have a lot when you grow up it's almost a virtue, because it makes you want to conserve," George says. "Our food was above average, we had decent clothes, we were loved and nurtured; we were never lacking in any respect. And yet, we didn't have a lot of material things."

While he was learning all of these values, George also found time to pursue a different kind of educa-tion, one taught by the tough hits and fast skating on the hockey rink.

"I enjoyed all competitive sports, but hockey was my favourite–I loved it," George says. "If I'd day-dream, I'd be Bobby Hull, born on January 3, number nine for the Blackhawks. He was my hero."

Though George and his brother skated a little on the dugout, they didn't play organized hockey until grade 7. George never officially played on a team until age 12. "I got a late start. But I enjoyed it. By the time I was 14, I was the leading scorer. My only claim to fame was that there were two guys who went pro (George Pasut and Willie Friesen) and I beat them both out for MVP in our league that year." By 16, George was playing on the senior men's team, and was the youngest player.

Pro hockey was an aspiration of George's, but it wasn't to be. However, like everything else he experienced, George took a lot of lessons from hockey. "A star hockey player might make $10 million a year," George says. "Do they work two years and quit? No, because they love the game—the action. They love the challenge and to prove themselves."

Leaving home

After high school, George decided to get to work—fast. Graduating on a Friday, he started his new job the following Monday at Smith-Roles Ltd., a shortline farm equipment manufacturer. George's plan was to work for a year, and then go to university.

After only a week on the job, his productivity was much higher than other guys on the line. He was building 26 cattle headgates a day compared to the average 19, and guys were asking him to slow down. Four months into his job experience, he was asked if he wanted to work in the office. George declined. "I said, 'No thanks.' I liked to work with my hands. I didn't want to work in an office."

The same day George got the offer for an office job at Smith-Roles, he came home to a message from what is now PotashCorp, where he had recently applied because they were offering $2.83 an hour–significantly more than the $2.25 an hour he was making at Smith-Roles. They offered him a job, and George accepted (even though Smith-Roles offered to match the salary if he'd accept their office job). He gave his notice, and went to work in the mines.

Not being aware of the nature of the potash business, George didn't realize that he would be laid off after a few months. George went to Canada Manpower to see what was available, assuming he could get a job at the Inco nickel mine in Thompson, Manitoba. In developing his resumé, he went back to Smith-Roles for a reference. "They said, 'Why don't you take that job we offered you before? We still have that for you.' My parents weren't in favour of me moving to a northern mining town–it wasn't exactly conducive to wholesome living."

George finally gave in and said he'd come back. Then he discovered that Smith-Roles weren't going to match the $2.83; they were only offering the original $2.25 he had been making there previously. True to his character, the plucky 19-year-old rose to the challenge with his well-honed negotiating skills. "I said, 'Hey, you told me $2.83.' They said, 'It's company policy.' I said, 'Okay, who makes policy? You might want to change it.'"

Smith-Roles stood its ground, so George offered to accept it, on one condition. "I told them I'd take the job for a month, then after a month they would have to pay me the new salary or fire me. After a month, they paid the new salary."

George started working at an office job in the purchasing department, where he had a lot to learn. "I started in January, and I remember thinking, 'I hope they don't fire me before spring–there will be construction jobs in spring,'" George recalls. "I didn't have confidence I could do it." But, by the time spring came, George was flourishing in the job.

Partners in fun and business, Dale Johnson and George enjoy skiing at Sunshine in Banff in 1984. They were joined on this trip by long-time friend, Phil Robinson.

George stayed at Smith-Roles for seven years. Out of 120 employees, he rose to become one of the top-ranked employees in the company. He left as the purchasing manager with a staff of three. He was 26 years old. "I had a tremendous learning experience there."

He also did two night classes at university–economics and business law–though he didn't complete a degree as he'd originally planned. The practical and action-oriented young man compared what he learned in his two classes to what he'd learned on the job, and decided that the latter was better. "I think education is good–and my kids go to university," George says. "I advocate for them to go. That said, I think education is highly overrated. So often, people have a degree and they feel they are really capable. The danger is you get a degree and think you know a lot. Life is a learning experience."

While working at Smith-Roles and taking night classes, George also dabbled in real estate. One night, he met some of his workmates at a bar for a few drinks after having just made $1,000 on a real estate deal–thanks to some quick thinking and innovative negotiating. His profit was the equivalent of two months' salary at that time. His friends called him "lucky." George responded, "Well, you can *call* it luck, but you've been here five nights in the bar, while, on

four of those past five nights, I've been looking at 30 properties, and am only here one night.' You *make* some of your luck."

Nobody worked harder at making his own luck than George. While working full time, he also had a handful of part time ventures–including a small insulating company, and an ongoing business of buying and selling motorcycles, houses, and cars–making money on all of them, and building his asset base. He lived in an apartment with a friend, rather than in any of the houses he owned, because it was cheaper to rent out the houses and live in the apartment. He bought his first house at 19 and, by 24, owned six.

Balancing work and play

Inheriting a gregarious nature from his father, George also made sure that he had time to socialize and travel. "My dad was a great advocate for traveling," George says. "He felt a person should get all the education in the world, and then make a trip around the world to complete it." When he was 19, George did a motorcycle trip to the 1974 World's Fair in Spokane, Washington. A year later, he went to Mexico with three friends. In 1975, he took a month-long trip to Europe with a friend. They had to be economical. "On the flight back, we only had a certain amount of money, and it was enough to either have a drink or watch a movie, not both."

On another trip, to Pakistan in 1987, George found himself in the town of Peshawar on the border of Afghanistan. At the time, it was a staging area for guerrillas organized by Osama bin Laden, who were fighting the Russians for control of Afghanistan.

The U.S. was backing the mountain tribes, called the Mujahadin, by supplying them with equipment and arms. George borrowed a Russian machine gun from a store, and dressed in the uniform of the Mujahadin to have his picture taken, just for fun, and to mark yet another adventurous occasion.

When it came to travel and socializing, George says his feeling was not to work until you retire and then travel. "Dad says, 'Give me the flowers while I live, not on my casket! I totally agree."

"I enjoyed life a lot at that time," George says. "I was the black sheep in my family. I partied pretty hard–wine, women and song were part of my repertoire. I played hard and worked hard. I definitely didn't miss out on life."

In retrospect, the self confessed "wild guy," who grew up in a Mennonite home and is now a practicing Christian, doesn't advocate any of the things he did during those younger years. But he does vote for balancing work with other aspects of life.

One night at a co-worker's party, George met Bonnie Bennett. George was organizing a chartered ski trip for 20 friends, and Bonnie was invited along. The trip proved to be the foundation for a relationship between George and the young registered nurse who worked at University Hospital in Saskatoon.

George found a counterpart in Bonnie, whose parents were English and Ukrainian. "We're quite opposite," George says. "I'm quite social; she's a bit more private. I'm more organized and neat than she is, but she's artistic, and I'm not. She worries about things; I don't. She's more risk averse than I am. She'll maybe back off from a challenge. I love a challenge. We really complemented each other."

With their relationship blossoming, and George's career going well, the stage was set for the next big move.

The evolution of Grandwest

In 1978, two years before he was to leave Smith-Roles, George got an offer from long-time friend and co-worker, Dale Johnson. A professional engineer who had left Smith-Roles, Dale, with another group, had started Senstek, which built electronic weigh scales. "Dale phoned one day–wanted to see me about business," George says. "I assumed he wanted me to come and join Senstek thinking I might work in the purchasing area."

The two met at the Travelodge, and Dale finally told his friend that he had sold his partnership in Senstek. George was more than a little surprised. After a couple of beers, Dale suddenly said, "Well, do you want you to go in business with me?" George replied, "You got anything in mind?" Dale said, "Nope."

But George liked the idea. So, over the next year and a half, they began searching for their own venture. When they had settled on an approach, George left Smith-Roles. In typical George fashion, when he made a move, it was a big one. On Thursday, April 3, 1980, George quit his job. The next day was Good Friday.

Adventurous George in Pakistan in 1987, dressed as a Mujahadin, and holding a Russian machine gun.

131

George and Bonnie in October 1978. George married and started a new job all in the same weekend.

"On Saturday, Bonnie and I got married. Sunday was Easter, and on Monday I had a new wife and new job."

George credits Bonnie with helping him make the decision to leave Smith-Roles. "She had lots of confidence in me," he says. "At the time, it was the biggest decision I'd ever made. For example, I made an offer on a building last week for $4.8 million. *That* was no big deal. Leaving my job back then was *everything*—it was my whole being. It was my income– a good job that paid well; I had a lot of responsibility. I felt I was very fortunate for a 25-year-old." But instinctively, his new wife knew he was ready to go out on his own. "Bonnie said, 'You should do it now.' She had an income. We weren't destitute. And, she was right."

After a honeymoon, during which he read a book called *From Failure to Success in Selling* to prepare for his new role as a salesman, George got straight to business with his new partner, Dale. They'd decided to sell shortline farm equipment, complementary to products manufactured by their former employer. Their first product was a fire extinguisher for combines. They also bought some property lots at Blackstrap Lake, did some development, and sold them at a profit. But neither of these activities was sustainable year round.

"Selling farming equipment was okay in the summer, but nothing happened in winter," George says. "So we looked for something else to sell farmers to supplement our summer income."

The original mission of Grandwest was to be a distributor of shortline equipment, rather than a retailer or manufacturer. "We didn't want to have to wait for customers to come in," George says, "and we didn't have the capital to build an expensive factory. We had three products for summer, but still needed something for winter."

They saw running boards on pickup trucks and bought 20, which sold immediately. They brought 20 more in, and, in a year's time, half of their business was pickup accessories. In their first year, they did $300,000 in sales.

Sometimes you *do* get lucky

In 1982, there was an accident in Florida where a vehicle was involved in a side collision. The running board was pushed into the gas tank, and the vehicle caught on fire. General Motors promptly decided that vehicles shouldn't have running boards.

Some saw this as a crisis in running board sales, but the Grandwest guys saw it as an opportunity on which to capitalize. "The factory we were getting our accessories from had 2,000 sets of GM running boards in stock," George says. "They were offered to four distributors in Canada, one of which was Grandwest. We got 500. Dealers still wanted them, and we sold them so quickly that we contacted the other three distributors, paid commission to them and sold a bunch more. It opened our eyes to what kind of market there might be."

George remembers the first year–taking to the road to call on dealers, selling a few pieces and coming back to ship products. At first, George was worried he wouldn't be a good salesman, just as he'd worried he wouldn't be able to do the purchasing agent job at Smith-Roles. "I was so embarrassed," he says. "Rather than go north, to communities I knew–I went south, where I knew nobody–to practice my selling. I did that for weeks. Then, back in the office, the phone would ring. Someone had bought something, wanted another one, or had an issue with it. We hadn't experienced that before, because nobody knew us."

Before long, the phones were ringing regularly, and George and Dale knew they needed to order more product. The next step of growth became obvious. "First, we stored the fire extinguishers in my apartment. Then we used Dale's porch, outside his trailer. We joked that he had the only 'warehouse' in the trailer park." Clearly, they needed more storage space. They found 1,000 square feet in a shared storage bay, which rapidly grew to a second and then a third bay until they had 6,000 square feet. When they got to the second bay, they bought out a similar-sized competitor.

Not all smooth sailing

Earlier, in 1981, they had a supplier from the U.S. who raised their prices 20% overnight, which was partly due to a flagging Canadian dollar. Costs went way up–and Grandwest suddenly found themselves unable to be competitive.

They needed a Canadian source, and found one in Ontario. Grandwest approached them to purchase their running boards, but the company declined, saying they had two distributors in Saskatoon already. George dusted off his negotiating skills. The problem was that each were distributors doing $60,000 or more annually, and the manufacturer didn't want to take any risks with those companies. George said, "Don't you want a better customer than that? I'll give you an order for $70,000 all at once." George knew he had to rock the boat; take a chance. "I knew we couldn't do that, but I also knew they couldn't ship that much at once, so it was a pretty safe bet." The bluff worked.

"That made them take a second look," George says. "They said, 'We'll sell to you–but we'll private label the product for you.' That was an absolutely pivotal moment. We would've died otherwise. It was the backbone of the company at that time. We needed that product."

The manufacturer made Grandwest a distributor, as well. In short order, Grandwest had grown and was more progressive than their competitors. "We worked a little harder, made more sales calls," says George. "We'd wear a jacket and tie and looked more businesslike. The others might be more mechanically knowledgeable than us–but we knew we'd never get a second chance at a first impression." By 1983, Grandwest was the manufacturer's main distributor. They bought out one of the competitors, while the other went out of business.

At age 15, George had told his mom, "I'm going to be a millionaire by 30 and then retire." In 1984, George turned 30. He had accomplished the first part of that promise, but wasn't ready for the second.

Grandwest has grown from only a few calls in 1980 to 2,500 per day in 2009.

Grandwest today

"I get accused of being very optimistic," George says. "I don't focus on mistakes. We've made a few, of course—getting poor quality product from another country that we just had to take a hit on, that kind of thing. But, overall, we've done really well."

He isn't kidding. Those first few phone calls answered by George and Dale have turned into 2,500 calls per day in 2009, handled by 25 salesmen. The three products have turned into 25,000 part numbers from 300 different product lines imported from the United States, China, Australia, Korea and elsewhere —making Grandwest Canada's largest distributor of auto accessories. George also now has a retail outlet, Tiger Automotive, on the Grandwest site in Saskatoon.

As of 2009, Grandwest has more than 5,000 customers (many of them customers since the early days), a staff of 100 and 130,000 square feet warehouse. Though they don't share their financial information, George will say that Grandwest carries a fully paid-for inventory and capital equipment of about $30 million. George also has business interests in real estate, manufacturing and farming.

Rod Thiessen, a friend since high school years and now a financial planner in Saskatoon, says there are many reasons for George's success. "Though one of his strongest skills is negotiation, you can't just have one skill to be as successful as he is, and I consider him to be one of the best businessmen I've ever met," Rod says. "For example, Grandwest has incredibly low number of bad debts for its size—so low the accountants can't believe it. He understands that the whole package needs to be done well to be successful. He doesn't shy away from dealing with anything; that's where his discipline comes in. He's a pretty special guy."

In 1991, Dale, George's partner of 11 years, announced his intention to retire. "It was a sad day for me," George says. "We had such a good partnership and friendship. But, he wanted to travel the world." George reluctantly bought Dale out in 1992. "We had the immense satisfaction of having been partners, starting from nothing, developing it enough that he could retire and we're still friends," George says.

Competitiveness a plus and a minus

"He is very competitive," Rod says. "But he's very respectful to others. George has been successful because of his people skills. He's interested in people's stories and lives. When you talk with him, he's right there with you."

Though George's people skills are strong, one of the most important lessons he has learned has to do with people—particularly with the people who work for him. "In the beginning, I pressed pretty hard for salesmen to be productive and I questioned them closely on what was going on," he admits. "I pressured them too much. Sometimes they might've needed some correction—but I've learned that when you have people, you work *with* them, and encourage them,

Grandwest has undergone five additions since 1989, currently comprising 130,000 square feet of warehouse, office and retail space.

build on what they're doing right. A new employee might do everything wrong in the first week, but you don't need to tell them about it–they'll know. Everyone makes mistakes. Sometimes people have a quality that's hidden–if you can bring it out, it will make the rose bloom."

So, the driving taskmaster has become the chief cheerleader of his company.

"I've learned instead of driving people to encourage them," he says. "The number one thing is people. The inventory we carry, buildings and equipment we have–*all* of these can be bought. But you need people with talent and attitude to make it work. You can't just 'buy' strong guys and give them some equipment and make a good hockey team."

"We started out as a two-man show, and I'm the sidekick now. I'm the employee advocate and human resources guy. It's the most important job I have."

Having fun with work

In the end, the "wild guy" of his youth returns in milder form. George and Bonnie delight in creating the best work atmosphere they can. Since 1983, they've had a generous bonus system that benefits every employee when the company performs; an annual year-end party that spans a weekend and involves all family members and a variety of unique non-cash perks.

In 2005, as part of Grandwest's 25th anniversary, the Reddekopps bought a cabin and announced that staff who had been with the company five years or more could book if for a week, for free. It became so popular, George decided to buy a second cabin.

With his love for interesting vehicles, George started a new annual trend in 1993 that continues today. He bought a vintage 1955 customized yellow Chevy truck, and told his employees that anyone who'd been with the company more than a year could sign up to drive it for a time. Over the years, he has bought a Hummer, a BMW X-5, and a '67 Chevelle SS396. For 2009, George bought two new Dodge Challengers, which are retro models that have been extremely popular.

Another year, he decided it had a "cool ring to it" to let employees say they drove the "boss' car," so he did the same with his own Mercedes.

On hot summer days, he might go buy a bunch of drinks, put them on ice, get on a forklift and drive around giving cold refreshment to folks working out in the heat. All in all, George's philosophy is simple. "Some things are priceless to people, and they often involve a simple human deed. If you can do a few priceless things once in a while, you're going in the right direction."

"Bonnie says I love the staff more than my own family," George says. "It's not the case, of course, but when she gets to questioning it, I'm close to getting it right."

The customized '55 Chevy truck George bought for his staff in 1993 started an annual trend that continues today.

Cas & Gord Broda
Digging deep

On a sunny June afternoon, George Shukin, a long-time welder at Broda Construction in Prince Albert, is working hard out on the equipment grounds. He's re-lining a rock truck box with new steel–cutting and fitting the pieces that he will later weld into place. At first, he doesn't notice the 80-year-old man approach and stop to intently watch his work.

When George finally looks up and sees the man, he quickly tromps down the tilted box to the ground. He takes off his work gloves and wipes one hand on his pants before offering it, and a big smile, to the familiar gentleman. "Hi, Mr. Broda!" he says. "Good to see you. What are you doing here today?"

Cas Broda shakes the welder's hand and says, "Good to see you too, George. I thought I'd better come down and take a look at this front-end loader Gordie bought at the auction. Make sure it's in good condition."

George nods. "Sounds like a good idea. Have a good day."

The elder statesman of Saskatchewan earth-moving waves and moves on toward the long line-up of bright yellow monster machines.

The encounter is brief, but is an example of the respect the employees of Broda Construction still have for the mostly-retired founder of the 52-year-old Broda Group of Companies, Cas Broda.

Son Gord, now president of the company, says this respect is born of the hard work and integrity that have been the hallmarks of his father's life, and are the legacy of the Broda Group of Companies that his father started with a single gravel truck, and a vision.

Cas Broda (right) still likes to show up now and then to check in on son Gordie (left), who now runs the earth-moving company his dad founded in 1957.

Cas gets his start

In 1904, Joseph Broda immigrated to Canada from Poland, settling with his family in Brandon, Manitoba, then moving to Saskatchewan to buy a quarter section for a dollar near Fenwood. The land was hardly a gift–full of stones, trees and brick-hard earth, it was back-breaking work to 'prove' it, or make it tillable. As a young man, Joseph met and eventually married Sophie Suwala from nearby Goodeve, and they homesteaded their own farm. They were tough–like Joseph's cousin and Maple Leaf goalie Turk Broda, considered one of the league's more rugged players.

Cas Broda was born in the hamlet of Goodeve, just west of Melville in 1929. Like many families during the Depression, the Brodas had very little money.

"Everything we earned we put into one kitty and Dad was king," Cas says. "There were three brothers and five sisters, and I was the oldest son. We lived on a small farm. We had a mixed farm–grain, cows, hogs, and sheep. It was real subsistence farming. Nobody had money in those days."

Cas excelled in sports (fastball and track) and school. A natural affinity for mathematics was to have its advantages as he continued his life journey. "No teacher could beat me in math," he remembers, "right from the beginning."

But, without money, Cas had to drop out of school after finishing grade 8 to work to help support the family. That didn't stop him from getting an education. "Because I couldn't get my formal education, I took correspondence," Cas says. "There were no jobs in Saskatchewan then, so as a young man, in 1947, I went to Ontario with some fellas to work in the wood industry. While the guys were reading Playboy magazines, I was studying."

Cas worked for nine years in the pulp industry in Thunder Bay. During that time, on one of his summer visits home, he met the girl who would become his wife. "We had these wiener roasts on Sundays where we would bring guitars, sing songs and play ball. One Sunday, there was a gathering at my brother in law's house and I met Marie through a mutual friend. It took a couple of years, but we finally got married."

Marie joined Cas for his last three winters working for the "old Scotchman" E.M. Hughes, in Thunder Bay, where she worked in the camp kitchen. Hughes had been urging Cas for years to invest in something, and start his own business. Eventually, Cas took his advice.

In 1957, after Hughes retired, Cas bought his first gravel truck and got started in the trucking business. His first job was to haul gravel from Regina–56 miles each way–for three months. Unfortunately, the material was rejected by the end user, so Cas never got paid–at least not in cash. "The guy didn't get paid for the job, so in lieu of cash he gave me an old loader," Cas says. "It didn't work very good."

His banker told him he needed decent equipment. He told Cas to go buy a new loader and to come see him if he had any problem making the payments. Cas bought the equipment, but never had to see the banker. He made all his payments on time.

To make the money he needed, Cas looked around for opportunity. Because of his experience hauling gravel, he considered expanding into the aggregate business. His opportunity came with the rural municipalities. "I was hauling logs for the government in Big River," Cas says, "and got into the RM business with a little screener. We had success keeping the RM jobs because we did good work for them, and I never charged them for the little 'extras' that other contractors did. We built up a good reputation. There was not a cheque I signed that was ever in question, and we always gave a little more than was expected of us."

Marie with Gordie and Shannon in 1965, during the Big River logging years.

Growing up on site

In October of 1960, Marie and Cas had a son, Gord–whom, to this day, Cas calls "Gordie." Two more children (Shannon and Robbie) were added to the family in the next few years, but it was Gord who would follow in his dad's footsteps in the construction industry. It started when he was a lad.

Gord spent a lot of time traveling with his parents to job sites before he was even in school. "I was a kid hanging around the job site," Gord says. "Dad's working on the job; mom's working in the camp kitchen. In the evenings, I got to play on the equipment. Of course nothing like that could happen today. Kids can't even go on the job site."

Finally, the family settled into a 40-foot house trailer in Kamsack. Cas started a concrete business called "Kam-Crete" in town to help anchor the gravel-crushing business. Now making aggregate from crushed rock, he finally had an address, his own shop and an office. "I remember being at the shop when I was a kid," Gord says, "and bringing a couple of buddies in to help unload a semi-trailer full of cement bags into dry storage. I grew up in the shop or on a project. I liked being around the men. I was comfortable doing that."

It took two years, but Cas and Marie were finally married in 1952. Here they are on their 50th anniversary, in 2002.

139

On weekends, Gordie would go with Cas to job sites. While his father was operating the big machinery, Gordie would often fall asleep in the cab beside him, his head bouncing against the window.

Gord remembers the monumental day when his family could finally afford to leave the cramped trailer and move into a house in town. He was in grade 4. "It was a big event," he recalls, "and a big highlight of my childhood. Most campers are bigger than that trailer was, but it was what we knew."

In the summer of Gord's 13th year, he went to work. "It was my first job where I wasn't riding along with Dad, and Dad wasn't supervising at the site. I knew how to run equipment by then, and one day Dad just said, 'Get in this front end loader, get on the highway and head down to McNutt.' I was a reasonably worldly guy for 13, but I still didn't know where McNutt was. He said, 'Don't worry, Jim'll be behind you, but get going.'" And that was that. The gangly teenager got into the machine, started it up and headed south on the #8 Highway. Sure enough, he soon saw Jim in the rear view mirror–pulling up behind him in a truck, passing him and showing him the rest of the way.

That summer, the owner's son, young as he was, made his presence known. "I was out workin' like a man," he says. "I'd be up at 5 a.m. to start the front end loader by 6 a.m., and I'd work until nine at night. Then we'd service our own machines at night, so that's how I learned to do repair work."

He enjoyed eating at the restaurants with the crew and "Havin' the odd beer when you weren't supposed to."

A second substantial job that summer occupied the 13-year-old as the main loader operator on a project to load gravel into 17 semi-trailers. "Most kids would've been grumpy, but I was working with the men, getting dirty, and I was putting money in the bank. It was my formal introduction into the construction world, and I liked it."

By the mid-1970s, with the help of a very strong supplier and supporter from Calgary whose forté was selling aggregate and rock-crushing equipment, Broda grew to be a strong presence in Northern Manitoba, working on projects in Lynn Lake and Thompson. For nearly eight years, Cas and his crews worked in the worst possible conditions that Northern Manitoba winters could dish out. "It was so cold there," Cas remembers. "We never slept much. We worked around the clock, the whole winter." But Cas, who had worked in Northern Ontario winters when he was younger, wasn't scared off.

The first winter, the temperature stayed below -48°C for an unbearable 78 days. "We had a lot of trouble with fuel freezing," Cas says, "and it was winter fuel meant to be good up to -60°C."

Winter wasn't their only enemy–the bad weather made the treacherous muskeg and hilly terrain even worse.

Cas, Shannon, Robbie, Marie and "Gordie."

Under these conditions, equipment frequently broke down, and maintenance work was a constant activity. At one point, Cas desperately needed a larger capacity gravel crusher (worth about $300,000) to finish the work. Times were tough, and financing could be a problem, but the supplier immediately sent a crusher to the site, for what would turn out to be two months, without a paper ever being signed. Broda had established such a good reputation for honesty and integrity that the supplier wasn't worried. "Our word was, and is, sacred with our suppliers," Cas says.

The new crusher got them through the project, running day and night. "It made back its down payment in two months, and we ended up keeping, and buying the machine."

This ability to finance new and bigger equipment, and to take the risk to do so, was to become a distinct advantage for Broda over their competition in the coming decades.

And, while son, Gordie, was apprenticing at the heels of seasoned welders, earth-movers, loader operators and foremen on project after project, his dad's company was about to move into an arena that would catapult the small company onto the national business stage.

Workin' on the railroad

In 1976, Broda Construction started its first railroad ballast project for the Canadian National railroad (CN) at a little site that came to be known as Mile 61-Payuk Lake, between Flin Flon and Cranberry Portage in Northern Manitoba.

Railroad ballast, the rock underneath railway tracks, was produced at quarries, then loaded and hauled all over western Canada and dumped on the rail lines. It was needed for new rail construction, but the Brodas realized it would also be a long-term business to provide the rock for ongoing repairs and maintenance of the track.

Gord was 15 at the time, and worked on this project as a full-fledged employee for Broda. He enjoyed being there that summer, and remembers the excitement of arriving just in time to see the shiny new equipment being unloaded off the rail cars. "It was really a big step for the company," he says. "It was a new challenge, requiring new equipment, a much bigger investment, and it was very risky because the railroads had a reputation of being tough to work for. They had very rigid specifications. We had to wonder if we could make this product for them efficiently, and on time." Rock-crushing experts were brought in from Milwaukee, and the teenager soaked up every word of knowledge and advice they gave the crews.

There were many other projects going on at the time, which meant a lot of the work force wasn't available and it was difficult to get enough men for their project. So, even at his young age, Gord remembers being made to feel like one of the "main guys." "I found myself explaining how things worked to the

Railroad car on a spur line, awaiting loading of ballast material.

new hires. Since I'd been in all the early meetings with the experts, I knew what was expected," he says. Though Cas was often on site, Gord acted almost in the role of a "sub foreman" and, by summer's end, he was the main front-end loader operator.

Looking back on the massive impact of the railroad projects on Broda, Gord says, "Dad and I shared in our very first railroad project way back then, and now here we are in 2009 still going strong. We've worked for the railroads every year since 1976, and have grown to meet their needs while our work philosophy has not changed."

Bolstered by ballast

Today, Broda produces ballast by drilling and blasting bedrock in Ontario and British Columbia quarries, and then processing the blasted rock by putting it through rock crushers that break it down to the 2½- to three-quarter-inch size. Enormous stockpiles of the ballast material (300-400,000 tons at a time) are created at the quarry sites. The ballast material then gets loaded into rail cars and is hauled to projects all over Western Canada to be dumped and spread over railway tracks.

From 1976 to 1992, the railroad ballast work represented most of Broda's workload. Broda grew along with the railroads during a huge expansion in the 1980s catalyzed by the Grainline Rehabilitation Program–the Canadian government's subsidy program of upgraded transportation lines for grain through the Prairies. Pretty soon, Broda was running two ballast crushing spreads instead of one, and traveling farther and farther away–to Oxbow, Climax, Val Marie, Craik and McKague. This growth resulted in Ed Kerluke (Cas' brother-in-law) taking on a key role in the ballast crushing operations. Ed had been in charge of running the Kam-Crete side of the business for many years.

The work on the Prairies slowed when the upgrading program ended in the late '80s, but, having established a good reputation for working with the railroads, Broda continued to get work as far east as Kenora and Dryden, Ontario. They also found more work up Manitoba's Churchill line and at other locations.

Then, in 1992, an enormous opportunity presented itself. "There was a big burst of activity out west," Gord says, "and we were the successful bidder in Kamloops. It was our first venture out to BC."

As usual, the opportunity was tied to risk. "We were nervous. We'd heard some concerns that, being a very unionized province out there, we could run into obstacles we weren't familiar with." The project was also very big–perhaps Broda's single largest dollar value project to date. To pull it off, they'd have to face the project's own unique "elements of risk and cautions," as Gord puts it.

But, as with every previous challenge, Cas, Ed, Gord and their crews pulled off a successful project, which led to more and more work.

There was a lot of competition, but Broda was successful because they offered bottom-line advantages to builders that included investing heavily in equipment, constant improvement of processes (which either improved productivity or lowered costs), and excellent crews to do the work.

"Dad had developed a style of crushing aggregate," Gord says. "He always wanted to be on the forefront of technology. In the 1960s and 1970s, there were crude ways of crushing rock–what was called a 'jaw/roll' combination. Then along came cone crushers– they were a brand new technology. Dad saw the potential and brought them on board quickly, while others hesitated. He always believed in looking for new ways of doing things, and he succeeded at it."

With the new cone crusher technology, Broda could crush a stockpile of rock in six weeks that would take competitors three months to crush.

Their other major advantage was that weather and terrain were never obstacles to the hardened crews who had braved the worst, and survived.

A tough business

The railroads purposely choose Cambrian shield or mountain locations for rail lines because the basalt granite found there creates a stable foundation with a long life cycle compared to gravel. But that stability means that crushers have to deal with very dense and abrasive rock. For example, a conveyor belt dumping rock on steel would wear a hole in a matter of days. Broda knew how to maintain equipment on the fly, minimizing downtime and reducing maintenance costs.

"The investment was pretty huge to get into the railroad business," Gord says, "and it wasn't all perfect. But my dad was a visionary. He had the ability to see a better way to do something, and even if we ran into roadblocks, he'd problem-solve and we'd fix it. The manufacturers would fly up for a visit and really like how he had adjusted a piece of equipment to make it work better, or last longer. I wouldn't doubt it if some of his Dad's ideas made it back into their production lines."

Improvement in crushing techniques led Broda into doing the same for drilling and blasting, until they were finally able to do both, which led them to even more work. In this arena, too, they found better ways to do it. "We found a more efficient and cost saving way to do drill-blast (another advantage) and then we crushed and drilled better," Gord says. "When we became the masters of our own drilling and blasting it allowed us to economize by spending a bit more on the drilling side–even 10 cents a ton will save you, maybe, 50 cents a ton on the crushing side."

The result of their ongoing search to increase efficiencies meant Broda got 85% to 90% of the railroad tenders at the time. "We captured those projects, regardless of the competition," Gord says. "We were getting the lion's share."

Gord credits his dad, himself and the people working with them for the culture created at Broda. "They were very good men," Gord says. "They'd make suggestions about changes we could make based on what we'd learned on the previous jobs." Today, we call that 'continuous improvement.' In those days, it was just about increasing production efficiencies.

"Those are qualities of my dad's I still admire," Gord says. "He was always production oriented. He'd be at coffee break, doodling on a napkin. He'd do some figuring, then say something like, 'If it's doing 300 tons an hour, and we can get it to 350, can you imagine what that would mean?' Or, 'If we went to the next size bigger truck, wait a sec … here!' He'd toss the napkin at you, point at it and say, 'We'll be ahead of the game if we do that.'"

Gord says it's a philosophy that he uses with all the people under his leadership.

The Brodas have seen a real evolution of a very successful partnership with the rail industry. Strong relationships were built over time, and eventually led to longer-term contracts, rather than the typical one-project tenders for Broda. Today, Broda interacts with the railroads on a regular basis. "We're involved in some of the planning, and we operate more like a partner than a sub-contractor," Gord says. "To some degree, Broda's been a partner longer than many of their own employees. Working for the railroads has been my life."

They've put a lot of energy into building that relationship. "To our credit, we've worked very hard, responded to their every demand," Gord says. "There have been hardships–changed plans, times when they've shifted gears in the middle of a project, or there's been an emergency. We've responded to their every need. We've always achieved delivery deadlines, always had materials.

"People look at competitive pricing–we can be counted on–we haven't let them down, and they put a significant value on that. In more than 30 years, we've never failed on a project."

Gordie and wife, Barb, met at her dad's Flin Flon Acklands store while on a job in 1982. By this photo in 2000, they'd been married 15 years.

144

There's more to life than work

In 1982, Gord met Barbara James, who was working in her father's Acklands hardware store in Flin Flon, Manitoba, while Gord was on a nearby job site. A summer romance struck up. Gord had started studying business at the Southern Alberta Institute of Technology in Calgary, and found out that Barb was studying to be a nurse at the University of Alberta, just up the road in Edmonton. By the next year, 1984, Gord had transferred to the Northern Alberta Institute of Technology in Edmonton. He and Barb married in 1985. A year after they both graduated, they moved back to Kamsack and Gord went back to work for his dad.

"When school was done, it didn't take me very long to say, 'I need to get back to the construction world,'" Gord says. "I got right back into the trenches and, shortly after that, I transferred into the management side of the business."

With his company experience, and business education, Gord was well positioned to become a true partner with Cas in taking Broda to its highest level yet–the big leap that would lead to the Big Dig.

Broda crews work in frigid winter conditions on the Big Dig, including several blizzards, one of which stopped work because of white-outs.

The Big Dig

In the early '90s, the railroad work had started to level off, and Cas and Gord were looking for new opportunities. They had all this big equipment–what else could they do with it? In 1993, the first part of the answer came to them in the form of a frenzy of excitement around the building of the uranium industry in Saskatchewan.

The rock-crushing Broda joined forces with an earth-moving company called Brent Construction out of Prince Albert, and Snake Lake Construction from Pinehouse, and together they bid on Cameco's McArthur River mine project. It was a marriage made in heaven. Gord moved his family to Prince Albert in 1994 to grow the new division. When the owner of Brent decided to retire the next year, Gord bought him out–creating a new division of the Broda Group of Companies called North American Rock and Dirt (affectionately referred to as "NARD").

With a real focus on the Saskatchewan North, and a strong 15-year relationship with Rene Rediron of Snake Lake Construction, the Broda team has worked for Cameco and Areva on most of their mine sites. They worked on gold mining properties, on PotashCorp projects and helped at Meadow Lake on the Tolko Industries project. They also did work for Sask Highways and the Alberta Department of Transportation.

"The projects became bigger and bigger, and we had to put a lot of capital into equipment to be able to compete for those projects." Again, Broda risked large investments into more and bigger equipment. NARD became Broda's biggest area of growth and, in 15 years, it grew into the largest earth-mover in the province.

"We got into a business where there were a lot of competitors," Gord says, "but again, we have the capacity to do jobs others don't want to do. Lots of companies prefer the South, there aren't a lot of complications–it's flat.

"We look forward to big mine projects. We're not scared of the North because there are rock, trees, muskeg. We've got the opposite attitude–give us a tough job–that's where we shine."

And, when it came to the Big Dig, they would need all that winter and Northern experience, all those good people and all that equipment. "It was one of the most complicated, toughest jobs the province had ever seen," Gord says, describing the 10-month project starting in October 2003. The challenge was to deepen Regina's man-made Wascana Lake, originally built in the 1880s. "The Big Dig was a collection of all our resources," Gord says. "Under the guidance of project manager, Russell (Rusty) Clunie Jr., we combined all of the best people and equipment from all our companies. It's a good example of being able to commit a large amount of resources–we *do* have the horsepower to get the job done."

145

Citizens of Regina thank Broda for its work on the massive Big Dig, which became a community spectacle for months.

Along with Dominion Construction and Clifton Associates, Broda Group of Companies took on the ambitious $18-million project. The problem was that the man-made lake had filled in over the decades, becoming a swamp in which people could no longer swim or boat, and a cesspool that sent up a brutal odour at the spring thaw from a winter's collection of goose dung.

What nobody could anticipate was that the project would become the city's top tourist site, for both Reginans and visitors to the city.

As Bob Hughes wrote in his book on the Big Dig: "Every single day, hundreds of people would go through the park to stop and watch the amazing procession of men and heavy equipment peeling the bottom off the lake. The workers themselves became celebrities, with people waving at them, holding up signs on the bridges, saluting them or taking them food. The work went on 24 hours a day, seven days a week and when it was finished, the citizens of Regina had developed a new pride in their newly-enhanced park."[1]

The entire lake was drained in a few days, and the massive amount of Broda equipment was paraded onto the site via 75 semi-trailer loads. Using a fleet of 22 rock trucks, with tires as tall as the men operating

them; nine track hoes (one shipped from Belgium that, alone, was worth $1 million); and more than 150 Broda crew working in non-stop 12-hour shifts, they began their work. More than $1 million was spent on fuel alone.[2]

Over the next five-month period, they faced a multitude of seasonal obstacles like frigid temperatures and one blizzard that shut down the entire region. And, there was the relentless march of time… Their work had to be completed before the unpredictable spring runoff–when millions of gallons of water would come rushing back into the lake bed, whether they were finished or not.

By mid-March, they had moved more than 1.5 million cubic metres of soil.[3] Once again, Broda came through on a project that tested every inch of their capacity, nerve and skills.

Following in footsteps

With the growth of Broda Construction, NARD and Kam-Crete, the Broda Group of Companies has become a mature and influential force in the construction industry in Canada. What began with 30 employees has grown by more than 10 times to more than 400. The Big Dig, alone, used 150 staff. It's definitely beyond anything Cas Broda had in

Broda says they've never seen community cheerleading of a construction project on this scale.

Today's Broda Construction headquarters in Prince Albert.

mind when he started his one-truck operation. "No, I never thought it would get this big," he says quietly, with a momentary look of wonder.

"When I first got into management, after school," Gord says, "I think the Broda entity was pulling in around $6-$7 million per year in the mid-1980s. Today, collectively, we're probably looking forward to in excess of $65 million." And the growth opportunity has never been this strong, he says. They anticipate moving up to $100 million a year in the next five years. They literally don't know how to stop growing. "It just evolves," Gord says. "Dad and I just keep asking ourselves, 'Are we keeping our people working?' and, 'Are we doing good work?'"

Where in the beginning they were once striving to do $1 million a year, single projects of that size are now considered very small, and are rare. A brand-new mining project will yield $20 million for Broda. "We can tackle it with confidence," Gord says. "We have a good team. We have no fear—I know we're going to do a great job." With that kind of confidence, and the track record of Cas and Gord Broda, it's hard to imagine them doing anything else.

The possibility of a third generation of Brodas carrying on the family tradition is a good one. Gord and Barb have three children of their own—two sons and a daughter, just as Cas and Marie had. What will Gord tell his kids about being successful? "Probably three things," he says. "First, and my father did it, and I did it—is to work hard and have integrity. Second, is to understand that at the end of the day, things don't just happen—you have to make them happen. I already tell my kids this. Too many people think things just happen by luck. There is no luck.

"From the outside, people think it must be easy. No…it's pretty hard work–you've got to be organized. You've got to be on your game every morning, work smart, and work hard."

And, finally, Gord will tell them not to be afraid to get their hands dirty now and then.

Though Cas Broda, who started it all in 1957, is mostly retired now, he co-manages a 5,000-acre farm with his youngest son, Robbie. "Dad's favourite thing to do is to have a tea and a sandwich, get on the tractor and go cultivate some land," Gord says.

"I came off the land," the elder Broda says, "and I love to see things grow."

And, he still checks in on son, Gordie, frequently, inspecting equipment, discussing a new project and offering his wisdom. He's the best role model a son could have. "I've been with my father my whole life," Gord says. "I have never, not once, had a job end and hear Dad first ask, 'Did we make money?' His first question was always, 'Did we do a good job?'

"Dad has taught us all that the most important thing is to do a good job. The rest will take care of itself."

147

Bill & Irma Smith
The couple that really cooked

They finish each other's sentences. They are comfortable co-storytellers, not surprising after their 49 years together as a couple, and one of Saskatchewan's most successful entrepreneurial teams.

"I emigrated from England with my family in 1953," Bill Smith starts.

"When you were 15," wife Irma Smith adds.

"I was a bricklayer," he continues.

"You became a bricklayer when you got here," she clarifies, "and your brother became a plumber."

"Having served five years in the Army and returning to find his job taken, my dad was disillusioned after World War II," Bill says. "He specialized in natural gas, and there was a lot of interest and opportunity for development in the Canadian Prairies. His brother in Neepawa, Manitoba…"

"…who was the mayor of Neepawa at the time and knew what was going on in the province," Irma interjects.

"…convinced my dad he should come to Saskatoon," Bill continues. "He was hired right away by the Department of Labour, and a few years later he wrote the Saskatchewan Gas Code that we still use today."

Irma goes on. "They had very little when they came here, and there were six children to support. Bill and his brother couldn't go to school, because they needed to go out and work to help pay off the family debt."

Bill nods. "Then my dad got transferred to Regina, to the head office, in 1957. I stayed in Saskatoon, and lived with a friend's family."

Bill and Irma Smith, in front of one of their properties, Saskatoon's Days Inn, have been the "dream team" from the get-go.

Dream team from the get-go

This is a story of fate, teenage sweethearts and a small coffee shop that went from making $40,000 in its first good year, to a catering enterprise that would top more than $10 million in annual gross sales by 2002–the year the Smiths decided to get out of catering and into their next venture–the hotel business.

Bill and Irma Smith were the "dream team" from the get-go. "From the beginning, we just clicked together," Bill says of his 48-year business partnership with his wife. They had the same values, and a shared vision. They were both hard workers, and willing to make sacrifices. They were the perfect pair to go into business together.

Bill and Irma met in 1956, hanging out with a mutual group of friends from Nutana Collegiate, where Irma was a student. Bill's mother went to the Nutana Bakery on Broadway each weekend to buy fresh bread. Bill tagged along, and it was there he first saw the vivacious Irma, whose parents owned the bakery. They were of German descent and, having both emigrated from Poland in the late 1920s, met later in Saskatoon and married. In 1951, they built the bakery, which they operated for 25 years, and which remained in the family for 55 years. Irma was born in Saskatoon, and had worked at the bakery after school and on weekends. Bill admired her hard work, and also found her attractive.

"I fell in love with her buns," he quips.

Irma smiles patiently, having heard this line a few times.

The two dated for four years, and married in 1960. Their original plan was to move to San Diego, where there was a project to build 10,000 homes on a U.S. Navy base. Bill had become a foreman bricklayer, and they needed men like him on the project. "We had our immigration papers approved," Irma says. "Then a letter came saying Bill would have to sign up to go into the U.S. Army. Irma's parents suggested that we stay in Canada, and buy a coffee shop they knew was for sale."

The shop was called the Green Court Snack Bar, and the young couple decided it was a good opportunity. Irma had some business and food service experience from the bakery, from attending a business college and from working stints for an accountant and at University Hospital in 1959-60. They were both raised to be hard workers, and most importantly, they both say, they had no fear. With $7,000 in loans from their parents and the balance from the bank, the Smiths bought the Green Court and started their first entrepreneurial adventure in 1961. "It had 15 stools and a counter," Irma recalls. "We battered our own fish for fish and chips, and peeled many pails of potatoes, by hand, for fries. Coffee sold for 10 cents a cup and cigarettes were 35 cents a pack."

Their first objective was to pay back the loans as quickly as possible. To do this, Irma worked days at the coffee shop, and Bill worked at the bakery. They'd meet for supper together, then Irma would go home, and Bill would head off to the coffee shop to work until 11 p.m.–a long day for Bill.

"We paid our parents back very quickly," Bill says. "Our philosophy was to make sure our suppliers were paid, the staff was paid and our commitment to bank loans was paid. If there was anything left over, it was ours. And sometimes there wasn't. Sometimes, we just barely ate and paid the mortgage. There was nothing else." This ethic of paying back loans quickly and paying suppliers on time was to become a hallmark of their financial dealings, and one of the most important factors in their ability to grow later. "Those relationships become critical. Your history makes a difference when you go back later and say, 'Now we need this amount to expand.'"

The young couple struggled through the early '60s. To add to their revenue base, they began offering concession services at various venues. Their first concession was with Royal American Shows for the weeklong Saskatoon Exhibition. Then, they added a concession at the stock car races on 8th Street.

At the same time, they were expanding their family–with the birth of their first son, Curtis, in 1962 and daughter, Cherryl, two years later.

In 1965, an office building, called the Diamond Industrial Centre, was being built on 33rd Street. Even with two young children and a demanding business, the Smiths saw a golden opportunity. They leased space there, opening Williams Restaurant and, later, William's Catering.

Learning on the job

An early learning experience came with the purchase of a concession at the Exhibition. The Exhibition management insisted on payment in advance. "We thought at the time that they didn't trust us," Irma says.

This fair concession stand was their first venture with the Exhibition in the late 1960s.

"We were so young [23 and 24] and they didn't know if we knew what we were doing." However, they later realized that everyone had to pay in advance.

The first year the Smiths had their concession, they put in 18-hour days, seven days a week–with no breaks.

"We thought we did so well," Irma says. "We were so excited that we gave all the staff bonuses. It ended up there was nothing left for us." Bill says that was their first important lesson. "Bonuses come *after* everything else is paid." They quickly note another important fact. "When we started our restaurant in the industrial area, we were only busy from 7 a.m. to 3 p.m.," Bill says. "We had this big expensive kitchen, rent and a [home] mortgage to pay."

"We needed to make ends meet, so, we started doing Sunday 'smorgs,'" Irma says, laughing. "We'd get university students who hadn't eaten all week. They'd come and eat us out of house and home. They'd have eight glasses of milk, five or six desserts. After the first year, we decided to give it up because it just wasn't profitable for us."

Williams Restaurant opened in 1965, and they later added the catering operation.

BEVERAGE

DESSERT

Some of the 1,200 athletes at the 1971 Winter Games who lined up for meals served each day for two weeks by Williams Catering.

Having successfully handled the catering for the Diamond Industrial Centre's grand opening, and with space to seat 150 people, the Smiths began catering to small weddings and bowling banquets. As they got busier, they started catering out to halls.

That same year (1967), their third child, Grant, was born. Juggling business and family commitments, and looking after three kids, kept the Smiths on their toes. "We were so busy in business during that time," Bill recalls. "I remember one day when there was a big snowstorm, and none of the staff could get to work at the restaurant, but customers showed up. I made it in, and I needed Irma there."

"The city was shut down," Irma continues. "I had the kids with me in the car. There was only one lane of traffic. You could hardly see; mounds of snow were everywhere, but we made it. I worked serving customers all day, Bill was cooking and the kids played in the small back office."

Despite their youth, the Smiths' reputation in business was growing. In 1969, at age 31, Bill was made president of the Saskatoon Restaurant Association, representing about 25 restaurants in town. The 1960s and 1970s were a boom time for the restaurant and catering industry, and the Smiths were handling 10 to 15 events every weekend. "In those days, people spent money on socializing," Bill says. "Not like today."

"We'd split the city in half," Irma says. "We had head banquet girls that handled each event, and Bill and I would split up and oversee different events."

"We never looked at the clock or a calendar," Bill says. "Our business was to *cater* to people. We were out to please them, so we made *sure* we got to every event, so people would be comfortable that everything was being looked after."

In 1971, they got their first major single event contract with the Centennial Auditorium, to cater for the Canada Winter Games. It was a massive test of their capabilities. They were to provide three meals a day for 1,200 athletes for 14 days in the large catering halls of the auditorium. An immense amount of planning went into the project, including the preparation of a thick manual on how everything was to run.

Their success with that event led to a 10-year exclusive catering contract with the Centennial Auditorium.

The mid-1970s saw continued success, and as the Smith children reached their early teen years, they started working in the family business. "The kids worked for us through high school," Irma says. "We'd hire their friends too. Our sons' friends would do truck driving and hauling, and our daughter's friends would set tables. They liked having spending money at their age, and had fun making it."

The Smith team was working smoothly, and was ready for something bigger. It came in the form of a project that proved to be one of their greatest challenges, and taught them a lesson in the precarious world of pricing competitive bids.

Battling the number bulge

In 1976, the Smiths entered new territory by bidding on a major contract for the Dundurn military camp, just outside Saskatoon. The tender indicated the job was to serve 45,000 meals over the summer.

"We won the contract because we had such a good price," Bill says. "You can offer better pricing on large volumes. But when we got out there, we realized they'd exaggerated the numbers to get a low price; there weren't as many people out there to serve as they had told us there would be."

Additionally, sometimes there would be food prepared for 1,200 people, and *nobody* would show up to eat. "They'd decide to go on maneuvers at the last minute on a Sunday without informing us in advance, and we'd be left with all that food," Bill says.

The situation was critical.

"We discovered that two previously contracted caterers had gone bankrupt under similar circumstances," Bill says. "We knew we needed to deal with the issue, or we would go broke."

The Smiths called in reinforcement in the form of their accountant from Price Waterhouse, Jack MacDonald, who pulled no punches with the generals flown in from Ottawa to meet with the Smiths over the contract. "After we threatened to pull off the site, stating that they weren't living up to the contract, the officials finally agreed to a reasonable and realistic percentage of the meals to be paid for, based on 85% of the actual tender," Bill says. Their formula was used by the military in subsequent years.

One challenge met, the Smiths moved on to face another, this time in the form of serving royalty from Bill's homeland.

In Their Majesties' service

Canadians experienced a most exciting royal visit in 1980. Princess Margaret was touring Canada, and making a stop at Saskatoon's Western Development Museum for a 500-person banquet held in her honour. For Bill Smith, who had come over from England as a teenager and was building a business of service, it was a chance to serve both countries–figuratively and literally.

Williams Catering pulled off a flawless event, which led to more major contracts, including 1982's World Youth Baseball Championship in Kindersley, where they served 350 athletes from 10 countries for 12 days. Their success in Kindersley caused area

Her Royal Majesty at a Williams-catered state luncheon in Kindersley in October 1987 as part of the Queen's Royal Visit to Canada.

153

Always ready to go the extra distance, Bill and Irma dress in suitable garb to help Carlsberg launch their new beer as part of a national campaign in the early 1980s.

Member of Parliament Bill Knight to contact them in 1987 for an event that would mean even more to Bill than the Princess Margaret banquet.

Who trumps a princess? Only a queen.

For Bill Smith, the opportunity to serve Her Majesty The Queen and His Royal Highness The Duke of Edinburgh, in October 1987 in Kindersley was a "great honour."

It was also a great challenge–1,000 guests, a high-end menu and…well…*the Queen.*

The bulk of the food was prepared in Saskatoon and trucked to Kindersley, but the protocols for preparing and serving the Queen's meal were exacting. "We rented the hospital kitchen in Kindersley," Bill says. "Officers from Scotland Yard, the Mounties and

representatives from the Saskatchewan Health Department watched the food being prepared."

In the end, the Smiths impressed everyone. In a handwritten letter, Shirley Haddock, advisor to the Canadian Secretary to the Queen and coordinator of the federal luncheon, said: "I was very pleased with the luncheon. As I have said many times it was the best meal in Saskatchewan and perhaps on the whole tour."[1]

Busy with increasingly larger catering events, Bill and Irma realized they needed more space. In 1982, they began working on expanding their facility–a huge risk to take, as it was smack in the middle of a deep recession.

No fear

"It was a big risk. Here we were, in our early 40s, and we built this big building. We just thought, 'If anything happens, we're young enough to start over,'" Irma says. "We never *really* thought we'd fail."

By early 1981, there were 15 to 20 full-time food preparation staff working in the main kitchen, and 150 to180 part-time staff working banquets on weekends. Williams Catering had serviced more than 800 weddings across the city–in church basements, Legion halls and at the Williams Catering facility– often doing 10 weddings on Saturdays. During the Auditorium contract years, they simultaneously managed three to four banquet rooms and catered to many conferences and other events.

As the Christmas and New Year's holidays were the busiest time of the year, the Smiths don't recall any personal celebrations with family or friends, other than Christmas Day. "We'd work events all night, and come back at 3 a.m. to help the staff do dishes in the central kitchen. When they were little, our kids stayed at Granny and Grampa's; then, later, they worked right along with us."

The time had come for a leap to a facility that would allow them to maximize their ability to manage multiple events. They met with an architect to plan for a $500,000 catering hall that would seat 600 people, with a massive commissary kitchen that could produce food for thousands of people, as well as manage an in-plant cafeteria service for large companies.

Ever the conscientious financial managers, the Smiths turned back the first design from the architect that drove the budget to more than $1 million. "It was fabulous," Irma says, "but we said, 'No, no, *no*. We need to live within the payments we can afford.' We knew our limitations, and we stuck to them."

The plan was scaled back by another architect, who fit the project to the original budget, and Williams Catering Hall opened on June 17, 1981.

Financing had been arranged through Roynat Ltd., who were impressed with both the Smiths' history of paying off loans early, and a business plan that showed how they would cope should interest rates rise substantially during the loan period. For this plan, Bill and Irma again called on the help of their accountant and friend Jack MacDonald.

"Jack came to our house on a Sunday morning and said, 'Do me a feasibility study to show me how you're going to make this work.'" Bill says. "It was during the recession. Interest rates were 12%. We thought it might go to 15%. We found a government assisted program to pay 5% below prime and we tied in with that."

It was another brilliant decision, as interest rates during that time actually skyrocketed to 22%. If they hadn't been in a program that held their interest rate at 17% (which was still high), the Smiths might not have been able to make the payments. As it was, the $500,000 loan was paid off, amazingly, in just five years.

This so impressed Roynat that the company featured the Smiths in their 1984 national advertising campaign which ran in major newspapers, including Toronto's Globe and Mail. In their press release launching the campaign called *What this country needs is more people like…* Roynat President John D. Thompson, said: "The campaign, which says nothing about our own services, was developed in the worst days of the recession to draw attention to the fact that many small and medium-sized businesses found opportunity, despite bad economic times."[2]

Roynat's Saskatoon district manager, Keith Lacroix, said: "We chose William and Irma Smith because of their initiative and enterprise. They have made a real contribution to the region in terms of jobs and growth. They represent the best characteristics of successful small and medium-size business people: risk-takers whose skill and effort bring benefit to the community as well as to themselves. Communities all across Canada would have a hard time surviving without people like them."[3]

The catering staff is called out for applause by attendees at the Williams Catering grand opening in 1981.

WHAT THIS COUNTRY NEEDS IS MORE PEOPLE LIKE WILLIAM AND IRMA SMITH.

At an age when many young people are still in school, newly-weds Bill and Irma Smith were running a small coffee shop in Saskatoon, days and nights, seven days a week. After several years they expanded to a restaurant in the industrial section where there was no evening trade and began catering special events. William's Catering was born.

As the business grew, the Smiths were everywhere: in the kitchen, out selling, behind

The Smiths were featured in this national print ad campaign by financiers Roynat in 1984. They were chosen because they were "risk-takers whose skill and effort bring benefit to the community."

With the new facility, the Smiths moved into factory cafeteria contracts for the likes of Northern Telecom, SaskTel and Innovation Place to keep their staff busy during the weekdays. Within a year, they were sending staff out to do luncheons at plants of

300 to 400 people, Monday to Friday, and five to 10 banquets on weekends. They also started "out-catering" lunches to many corporate offices.

Then came another challenge; one that would take them out of Saskatoon, and up to the far reaches of Saskatchewan's North.

Creating jobs in the North

Within a year after opening their new facility, the Smiths won a contract with Eldor Mines for catering, managing housing for miners at a Northern mining site and janitorial services. It started at Rabbit Lake. The previous supplier's contract had ended, and wasn't being renewed. Eldor needed a new caterer, fast, and they liked the Smiths' track record. To enter this new arena, the Smiths had to create a new company, which they dubbed "IW Campsite Catering."

"We had two weeks to come up with a name for the new company," Bill remembers. "So we used the 'I' for Irma and the 'W' for William."

Irma says, "Because the old contractor was pulling out, they were taking everything with them. We had to go buy dishes, bedding, pans...everything. When we got up there, it made a big impression on the miners–everything they'd had before was old and used, and we brought all new things."

They also impressed Eldor with ideas about how to increase employment opportunities for Northern people, a long-time goal of the company.

"We moved in with a big Northern employee ratio idea," Bill says. "Before us, the caterers would send staff into camp for six to 10 weeks at a time. People didn't like that–they had to be away from their families for too long."

156

The cafeteria managed by IW Campsite Catering, the Williams' first venture in the North.

Noting that the miners themselves worked on a seven-day in, seven-day out schedule, the Smiths asked if Eldor could accommodate the hospitality staff on the same schedule. "We asked them if there would be room on the planes for our staff. There wasn't, but they liked the idea so much they changed to larger planes to accommodate it."

With multiple pick-up and drop-off points like Fond du Lac, Black Lake, Uranium City and La Ronge, the catering employees could get to and from their jobs at the camps much more easily. "Most of our employees were young people," Bill says. "They got camp fever staying too long. They didn't like being away from family and community, so the changes made an otherwise 'okay' job *really* good."

The Smiths had no problem attracting Northern people to the jobs and, before long, the Northern employee ratio at Rabbit Lake was 73%, more than double what it had been in the past.

The Rabbit Lake catering operation saw an annual payroll of $900,000, with $1 million in food supplies and $200,000 in cleaning supplies. Trucks brought in 20,000 pounds of groceries each week. Each month hungry miners ate and consumed 1,000 pounds of bacon, 12,000 eggs, 500 gallons of milk, 150 gallons of ice cream and 2,500 pounds of fresh fruit. By this time, IW Campsite Catering was bringing in $4 million in sales each year.

A joint venture

In 1988, a year after they'd built a mall in Saskatoon called Circle B Mall, Bill and Irma decided to retire from the social end of catering in the city, and moved their office to their new mall location. They sold Williams Catering to a young couple, just starting out–like they had been 27 years earlier. "We were both exhausted," Irma says.

They could now focus their entire attention on catering to the mining industry, which was growing in the North. Eldor had become Cameco, and Cameco had mines on aboriginal land. The bands were adamant about creating as much employment and business opportunity for Saskatchewan First Nations people as possible. So, to build on their 10-year success at Rabbit Lake, the Smiths came up with a new proposal for Cameco's biggest uranium mining site–Key Lake.

In 1991, they created a partnership with the La Ronge Indian band's Kitsaki Development Corporation. Their new company was called Six Seasons Catering. The La Ronge band held majority ownership (51%) and the Smiths held 49%. The company name was based on Wood Cree beliefs about six, rather than four, seasons–correlating to the six stages of growing wild rice.[4] The name also represented the continuous nature of providing service at a mining site, which operates on shifts 24 hours a day.

157

This unique venture was created without any government assistance, and was financed solely by the partners of the company–Kitsaki Development and the Smiths. "We [IW Campsite Caterers] became the management company," Bill says. "We managed everything from our head office in Saskatoon. We tendered contracts, did the accounting, payroll, menu planning and purchasing of supplies for the North, all from the city."

Working in the camps was a first job for many of the new staff, and part of the program Six Seasons Catering offered Northerners was on-the-job training for unskilled workers. In 1992, when the company was only a year old, it was selected as one of five finalists in the job creation category for the ABEX Awards of Excellence. The Smiths remain proud of this distinction.

With 10 years of experience under their belts at Rabbit Lake, the Smiths had become seasoned veterans of mining camp culture. As they had at Rabbit Lake, they managed not only food services, but also janitorial work, housekeeping and lodging coordination for the Key Lake camp; which was, at the time, the largest high-grade producing uranium mine in the world. Start-up costs in 1991 were $160,000 for essential supplies like bedding, dishes, pots and pans, a new truck, janitorial supplies and office equipment.

In the mid-1990s, more bands wanted to become involved in the company. Six Seasons Catering was renamed Athabasca Catering, and four more bands became shareholders.

Eventually, two mines (Cigar Lake and McArthur River) were added to the contract, for a total of four major mining sites. Athabasca Catering now had anywhere from 250 to 350 staff working in the camps at any given time. "We served up to 700 people three meals a day for 365 days of the year," Irma says of the enormous project. The Smiths' company sales topped $10 million a year in those prime years.

Their son, Grant, came back to work for his parents in 1991, and became heavily involved in the management company, eventually working his way up to become their "all sites" manager. He managed all the problem-solving with staff, ensured smooth running of the camps, and purchased all supplies for each site, eventually helping with contract bidding. "It was hard work, but he did a superb job," Irma says.

In 2002, Irma and Bill sold their shares in Athabasca Catering and retired after 10 years from what turned out to be a successful venture with Northern bands. The bands now own 100% of the company.

Wait, they're not finished yet

But the Smiths' definition of retiring is a little different than many others' might be. By "retire," they meant get out of catering–and build a hotel. They had a previously purchased parcel of land at a busy intersection in Saskatoon's North end; and were considering whether it was a good location for a hotel.

"Some people didn't think there was room for another hotel at that location," Bill says of the busy Idylwyld-Circle Drive interchange. "But I had been watching it for a long time. The Travelodge [across the street] was always full. I learned there were 60,000 cars a day going one way, and 45,000 cars the other way at that intersection. It was a *great* location."

"We're very proud of all of our children," says Irma of Curtis, Cherryl and Grant.

Though they had observed traffic patterns and watched the busy hotels in the area for some time, they weren't going to make a decision of that magnitude only on that information, and hired a research company out of Vancouver to do a feasibility study of the location. "After a *very* successful PKF[5] report," Irma says of the results, "we made the decision to build a four-story, 102-room hotel."

Next, they needed to find the right hotel franchise opportunity. They liked what Days Inn had to offer, and opened the Days Inn in Saskatoon in July 2001. They had built a large restaurant on the remaining piece of the land, and their next move was to woo the Tony Roma's restaurant chain into leasing from them. It was another feat many in the industry said they couldn't achieve.

Meanwhile, the Smiths' daughter Cherryl, who had taken classes in business and merchandising, had recently completed an interior decorating program in Vancouver. Her parents asked if she thought she could decorate their hotel. She not only decorated, but designed each room layout, and all furniture, lighting and fixture placement. She chose all the carpets, bedding, furniture and drapery. "It was a lot of work on her part," Irma said, "and she did a wonderful job." In fact, Cherryl was offered another job decorating a new hotel in North Battleford. She declined the offer, as she had come on board to co-manage her parents' hotel with her brother, Grant.

By 2005, the 35-employee operation was able to boast a more than 90% occupancy rate all year, which it maintains today. For its excellence, the Days Inn has won national accolades from Days Inn Canada, including Hotel of the Year, twice, and the Chairman's Award every year since it opened.

Though not in the family business, their other son, Curtis, has done well for himself as well, in real estate development in Whistler, B.C.

"We're very proud of all three of our children," Irma says. "They worked hard with us as kids, and shared in our success. We approached them when we wanted to get out of the catering business and asked if they wanted to stay in it, and they all said, 'No.' They grew up with it, and knew how hard the catering business was."

"Our banker said he understood," Bill says. "He said, 'Every night at supper, the kids listened to all the problems–staffing, logistics. When they grew up, they probably decided they didn't want that kind of life.' I think he was right."

But "that kind of life" was more than fine for the two confident young kids who had started out in 1961, knowing only that they couldn't fail; and that if they *did*, they would simply start over. They are, even to this day, active in the business world. In September 2009, Bill and Irma bought a newly-built, 94-room Holiday Inn Express in Courtenay, B.C. Their son, Grant, will move there to run the operation.

"You can do whatever you put your mind to," Bill says to young entrepreneurs these days. "You're young. Don't think of failure…Go for it!"

About the Prairie Policy Centre

As publisher of Birth of a BOOM, the Saskatoon-based Prairie Policy Centre, Inc. (PPC) is extremely pleased to have helped bring these 13 exceptional stories of Saskatchewan entrepreneurs to life. From the moment Norm Wallace brought the idea forward, the volunteer board of directors saw the importance of recording these stories for future generations.

After all, the Prairie Centre is an independent non-profit corporation dedicated to a free and prosperous Prairie Region. It strives to help people understand more about wealth creation, its relationship to their economic and social well-being and how public policy decisions affect the creation of that wealth. And, in a free and competitive market, entrepreneurship and innovation become the basis for wealth creation.

The policy centre takes wealth creation to mean growth in investment, jobs and population. It believes that entrepreneurship (taking innovative ideas and making them happen) in a free market environment will be pivotal to attracting investment and creating jobs in Saskatchewan and the Prairie Region as a whole.

The mission of the Prairie Policy Centre is to foster a greater understanding of wealth creation in order to shape public policy so as to maximize opportunities for everyone.

Policies for a Free and Prosperous Prairie Region

The centre carries out its mission by:

- maintaining a diverse membership that furthers its work by helping more people develop an interest in and knowledge of economic policy;

- examining current and emerging economic issues to identify those public policies that foster wealth creation and those which impede it;

- measuring, studying and communicating the impact of public policy decisions on investment, job creation, and economic growth;

- bringing expert insight about policy alternatives for the creation and preservation of wealth to the attention of the broadest possible audience; and

- acting as a catalyst for informed discussion and debate on topical public policy issues.

Since knowledge and a broad awareness of the potential effects of public decisions are fundamental to the development of good public policy, knowledge management is a core function of any policy organization. However, PPC Executive Director, Allan Evans, says it's not for the policy centre to tell anyone how to think or what to believe: Our job is to be honest brokers of good information.

PPC is funded solely by voluntary contributions from individuals, small business, corporations and organizations that share a common interest in making the Prairie Region a better place to live, work and prosper.

About the W. Brett Wilson Centre

The vision of the W. Brett Wilson Centre is to achieve pre-eminence in teaching, research, outreach and engagement. Since inception and subsequent approval on May 15, 2008, activities have been focused on building on these three pillars. We define entrepreneurship as innovative thinking coupled with disciplined action and we believe innovation can happen anywhere, in any form and by anyone. This is the essence behind the Centre and all its activities.

The mission of the Centre is to inspire excellence in entrepreneurship in every student on the University of Saskatchewan campus. The Centre coordinates entrepreneurship minors through the various colleges (i.e. Ag/Bioresource, Arts & Science, Edwards School of Business, Engineering, and Kinesiology) and we are building relationships to provide access to mentoring, coaching and networking to teach the discipline of entrepreneurship beyond the classroom. Preparing minds to create economic wealth, with an environmental and social consciousness, is the goal of the Centre.

Through its initiatives, the Centre will facilitate interactions and formation of informal networks among the student bodies including engineering, science, arts, business, politics, media and sports. In addition, we are constantly forming connections to the wider Saskatoon and Saskatchewan community, developing key partnerships that add relevance and enhance student experiences with opportunities for mentorship, growth, employment and wealth creation.

In Saskatchewan, it's an exciting time of change. Renewed interests are spurring on new collaborations and partnerships…and the newly formed W. Brett Wilson Centre for Entrepreneurial Excellence is positioned at the core of this renaissance.

It acts as the "front door" to entrepreneurship and we will strive through our initiatives to engage the minds of our students, inspire them, support them and educate them.

The Centre encourages our partners to give their time, talent or resources…all are welcomed and enrich a student's education, experience and helps accomplish our common goal of creating leadership excellence.

Guiding values of the Centre

- We embrace lifelong learning and the pursuit of knowledge.
- We embrace innovative thinking.
- We believe that innovation can happen anywhere, in any form and by anyone.
- We believe in courage and challenging the status quo.
- We believe excellence is being better today than yesterday.
- We value teamwork, people and their ideas.
- We value and promote integrity.
- We believe in creating wealth with a heart (social and environmental consciousness).
- We believe priorities guided by passion leads to a life of significance.

Centre activities

The Wilson Centre has exciting initiatives, creating opportunities for students and collisions with the business community. The "i³ idea challenge" student business plan competition, launched in September 2008, attracted hundreds of U of S undergraduate, graduate and post doctoral students with the opportunity to demonstrate entrepreneurship skills and innovative thinking. At Leadership Conference 2009, the top three teams were announced for the first annual "i³ idea challenge" and over $145,000 cash and prizes were awarded. Winners can be viewed at www.innovate.usask.ca.

The "i³ idea challenge" is a vehicle that was designed to create collisions among students on campus and between the business community and U of S students. It's about connecting the thinking with the doing and encouraging imagination, invention and innovation, the three 'i's of the competition. The results have indeed been exponential. I would encourage future students at the U of S to experience the competition and be part of a "rare breed" of students.

Sask INC (Innovate, Network, Create), an annual public innovation forum, connects business leaders, researchers, students and financiers from key economic sectors to discuss innovation opportunities and needs for Saskatchewan in two streams of strategic importance: natural resources and health.

With intense competition, along with rapidly developing markets and technologies, no one needs to be convinced of the importance of innovation. How to innovate is the key question. Dr. Richard Satava, head of surgery at University of Washington and Project Manager at one of the U.S.'s top-secret

Examples of two Wilson Centre initiatives for students and the business community.

research facilities delivered this year's keynote, providing innovation examples beyond one's imagination.

Sask INC was held on September 14 and 15, 2009 at TCU Place in Saskatoon and gave delegates, presenters and students the opportunity to participate in discussions on leading edge issues and on innovation in Saskatchewan. "Saskatchewan is full of opportunities and can lead the recovery from the current economic downfall through innovation and entrepreneurship," adds W. Brett Wilson, chairman of First Energy and co-honourary chair of Sask INC's innovation in natural resources stream. "We need to work together and leverage the greatest asset we have –our knowledge resources."

Sanj Singh, Director of the W. Brett Wilson Centre continues to use its initiatives, teaching and research to advance entrepreneurial thinking throughout the campus and Saskatchewan. "We are constantly looking for opportunities to build relationships and partnerships. We look forward to welcoming future students to the U of S and finding and building leaders. We are committed to creating innovative thinkers who can become the change agents for economic, social and/or environmental growth, sustainability and prosperity."

NOTES

Chapter 1

Birth of a Boom
Pride of place

Interviews
Herb Freidenberger.

Other sources

Employment Dynamics Report. (1999). Statistics Canada. Accessed via the Enterprise Saskatchewan website on October 15, 2009.

Enterprise Saskatchewan website. Accessed via www.enterprisesaskatchewan.ca/Small-Business on October 1, 2009.

Saskatchewan Fast Growth Study. (June, 1993). KPMG Peat Marwick Stevenson and Kellogg. pp. 45-46 and Appendix D, pp. 1-2.

Scholz, Al. (2000). Don't turn out the lights: entrepreneurship in rural Saskatchewan. Saskatoon: Saskatchewan Council for Community Development.

Small Business Page. Enterprise Saskatchewan website. Accessed via www.enterprisesaskatchewan.ca/Small-Business on October 1, 2009.

Wong, Queenie. (2009). Communities in boom: Canada's top entrepreneurial cities. p. 1-11. Toronto/Ottawa: Canadian Federation of Independent Business. Accessed via http://www.cfib-fcei.ca/cfib-documents/rr3091.pdf on October 20, 2009.

End notes

1. Defined by Statistics Canada as "those with less than $5 million in annual sales or with fewer than 50 employees."
2. KPMG Study.
3. Employment Dynamics Report.
4. Business Register.
5. Queenie Wong, p.3.

Photo credits
All photos courtesy of the Freidenberger and Paschall family collections. Chapter feature photo taken at Christopher Lake by Debra Marshall.

Chapter 2

Norm Wallace
Roots of a renegade

Interviews
Dale Boothman, Norm Wallace, James Waldbillig, Kent Smith-Windsor, Gerald Wuttanee.

Other sources

Adams, B.A. (1996, April 20). Inferno on 41st Street. *The Saskatoon StarPhoenix*, p. A1.

Evidence. (February 13, 2003). Standing Committee on Citizenship and Immigration, Government of Canada. (27th Parliament, 2nd Session). Accessed via http://www2.parl.gc.ca/HousePublications/Publication.aspx?Language=E&Mode=1&Parl=37&Ses=2&DocId=707087&File=0#Int-422457 on March 17, 2009.

GPC Capital Corporation website. Accessed via http://www.greatplainsofcanada.com/pages/norm.asp on November 20, 2008.

Martin, P. (1996, May 11). Fire showed construction owner new side of city. *The Saskatoon StarPhoenix*, p. D5.

Prairie Policy Centre website. Accessed via http://www.prairiecentre.com/Norm%20Wallace.htm on January 25, 2009.

VBine Energy website. Accessed via http://www.vbine.com/index.php?option=com_content&task=view&id=6&Itemid=7 on December 5, 2008.

End notes

1. Fontana, Joe. Standing Committee on Citizenship and Immigration.
2. Martin, Paul.
3. PPC website.

Photo credits
All photos courtesy of the Wallace family and Wallace Construction private collections, except page 10. Page 10 compilation is courtesy of The Saskatoon StarPhoenix.

Chapter 3

Herb Pinder
Play hard, work harder

Interviews
Herb Pinder, Sr., Herb Pinder, Jr., Gerry Pinder, Tom Pinder, Richard Pinder.

Other sources
Duff, David G. (2005). The abolition of wealth transfer taxes: lessons from Canada, Australia and New Zealand. [Abstract]. *Pittsburgh Tax Review*. Available at SSRN: http://ssrn.com/abstract=719744 or DOI: 10.2139/ssrn.719744.

Encyclopedia of Saskatchewan. Accessed via http://esask.uregina.ca/entry/pinder_family.html on February 11, 2009.

Government of Canada website. Accessed via www.canadianeconomy.gc.ca/english/economy/1947Leduc_Oil_Discovery.html on April 9, 2009.

Hockey Hall of Fame website. Accessed via www.legendsofhockey.net/LegendsOfHockey/jsp/LegendsPlayersByTeam.jsp?team=Saskatoon+Crescents on June 22, 2009.

7-Eleven corporate website. Accessed via www.7-eleven.com/AboutUs/Milestones/tabid/76/Default.aspx on July 9, 2009.

End notes
1   Hockey Hall of Fame website.
2   Encyclopedia of Saskatchewan website.
3   Government of Canada website.
4   Duff, David. p.118. At the time of the taxes, it was argued, "First, if wealth transfer taxes are to be maintained or reintroduced, the political costs of these taxes must be minimized. Crucially, basic exemptions must exclude small and medium-sized estates and be regularly adjusted for increases in asset prices. Where these exemptions do not fully relieve the burden on family farms and small businesses, other rules should provide for special valuation and deferral of tax so that these assets need not be sold in order to pay the tax."

p.105. "In his 1977 budget speech, British Columbia's Minister of Finance announced that the provincial succession duty and gift tax would be abolished…Later that year, the N.D.P. Government in Saskatchewan announced that it would repeal the provincial succession duty and gift tax."

5   The favour was to help Gerry successfully negotiate his contract with the Blackhawks. Herb called player agent Allan Eagleson himself to ensure the right terms, and asked his son to make the promise of returning to school when his hockey career was over.
6   The first Canadian 7-Eleven store opened in 1969.

Photo credits
All photos courtesy of the Pinder family collection.

Chapter 4

Spencer Early & Joe Bloski
Seeds of risk

Interviews
Joe Bloski, Spencer Early.

Other sources
Saskatoon Centurions: A century of success. (2007). [Supplement]. *The Saskatoon StarPhoenix,* p. 20-23.

End notes
1   An excerpt from a letter from Rolf Hagen of Hagen Pet Foods, Germany.
2   Centurions.

Photo credits
All photos courtesy of Early family and Earlys Farm & Garden private collections.

NOTES

Chapter 5

Gavin Semple
Dreaming big

Interviews
Gavin Semple, Shaun Semple.

Other sources
Brandt Corporate Profile (2009). Brandt Industries, Ltd.
Moen, Keith. (December 2003-January 2004). 2003 Business of the
    Year: Brandt Group of Companies. [Special issue].
    Saskatchewan Business Magazine, 21-27.
Saskatchewan Government website. Accessed via http://www.ops.
    gov.sk.ca/Default.aspx?DN=a4e9e20b-d74e-423c-8128-
    e53107c610c6 on March 12,2009.

End notes
1   Moen, p. 23.
2   Moen, p. 25.
3   Saskatchewan Government website.

Photo credits
All photos courtesy of Gavin Semple family and Brandt Group
of Companies private collections.

Chapter 6

Wendy & George Morris
Doing what has to be done

Interviews
Casey Davis, Wendy Morris.

Other sources
DeRyk, Dick. (1991). It was in him: the George Morris story.
    Yorkton, SK,Canada: Printers Features Inc.

End notes
1   deRyk, p. 24.
2   deRyk, p. 29-30.
3   deRyk, p. 30. Summer fallowing is a practice of not seeding a
    crop on a piece of land every few years to allow the soil to
    rejuvenate. Men from that area left in 1885 for the campaign
    against Métis leader Louis Riel, and returned too late for their
    regular spring planting. The next year, crops sown on the fallow
    land produced quantities nearly 20 times as big as non-fallow
    land crops.
4   deRyk, p. 39.
5   deRyk, p. 45.
6   deRyk, p. 65.
7   deRyk, p. 69.
8   deRyk, p. 118.
9   deRyk, p. 131.
10   deRyk, p. 135.
11   George had two strokes, in 1971 and 1978.
12   deRyk, p. 189.

Photo credits
All photos courtesy of Wendy Morris family and Morris Industries
Ltd. private collections.

Chapter 7
Kevin & Jerry Tell
Out of the ashes

Interviews
Shawn McMillan, Beryl Tell, Jerry Tell, Kevin Tell.

Other sources
City of Regina. (2007). Regina Heritage Walking Tours: Eight Self-Guided Tours of Regina's Built History. (4th ed.) [Brochure]. Regina, SK: Author.

Ghosh, C., Guttery, S., Sirmans, C.F. (1994). The Olympia and York crisis: effects on the financial performance of US and foreign banks [Electronic version]. *Journal of Property Finance*, 5(2), 5-46.

Newman, Peter C. (2008). Izzy. New York: Harper Collins Publishers Ltd.

End notes
1 Though the idea of mixing cinders with concrete had been utilized in other parts of North America at roughly the same time, it's unclear whether or how Jacob and Adam would have known this. Regardless, in addition to it being a vast product improvement and new on the Saskatchewan market, it was also pure entrepreneurial genius to acquire the material free of charge by offering to do CN a "favour" in getting the "waste" product off their hands.

2 Peter C. Newman, p. 211.

3 Ghosh, Guttery, Sirmans.

Photo credits
All photos courtesy of Tell Family and Cindercrete private collections.

Chapter 8
Wade Mitchell
Never say die

Interviews
Wade Mitchell.

Other sources
Battleford Regional Gen Web Genealogy website. Accessed via http://www.rootsweb.ancestry.com/~skbattle/Battleford/BattlefordObits.htm on February 19, 2009.

Hibbert, Joyce. (1985). Fragments of war: stories from survivors of World War II. Greenland Ordeal. Toronto: Dundurn Press, pp. 250-260.

End notes
1 Hibbert, p. 258.

2 Hibbert, p. 259.

Photo credits
All photos courtesy of Wade Mitchell family and ASL Paving private collections.

NOTES

Chapter 9

Ernie Poole & PCL Employee-Owners
Poole's people

Interviews

Paul Douglas, Michelle Gagnon, Kris Hildebrand.

Other sources

Graham, Shirley R. (2005). The PCL story–our first 100 years. Edmonton, AB: PCL Construction Ltd.

Webster's Dictionary. [Electronic version]. Accessed via http://www.merriam-webster.com/dictionary/family on June 10, 2009.

End notes

1   Graham, Shirley, p. 49.

2   Graham, Shirley, p.7.

3   Graham, Shirley, p.11.

4   Graham, Shirley, p.12.

5   Graham, Shirley, p.15.

6   Graham, Shirley, p.28.

7   Graham, Shirley, p.36.

8   Graham, Shirley, p.37.

9   Graham, Shirley, p.41.

10 Graham, Shirley, p.46.

11 Graham, Shirley, p.15.

12 Graham, Shirley, p.48.

13 Graham, Shirley, p. 53.

14 Graham, Shirley, p. 52.

15 Graham, Shirley, p. 56.

16 Webster's Dictionary.

Photo credits

All photos courtesy of PCL Group of Companies private collection, except pages 91, 92 and 99. Page 92 image produced, and provided, by Apollo Sheet Metal of Kennewick, WA. Pages 91 and 99 photos courtesy of the Poole family.

Chapter 10

Ron Carson
Into the sweet light

Interviews

Ron Carson, Mark Langefeld.

Other sources

American Petroleum Institute website. Accessed via http:www.api.org/aboutoilgas on May 16, 2009.

Bakken oil formation has industry gushing. *The Saskatoon StarPhoenix.* [Electronic version]. Accessed via http://www.canada.com/saskatoonstarphoenix/news/local/story.html?id=5f07f6b9-815f-4058-9e25-17fb0c61cd61 on May 25, 2009.

Byfield, Mike. (November, 2007). Bill Boyd: Saskatchewan's new energy minister wants long-term trust. *Daily Oil Bulletin.* [Electronic version]. Accessed via http://www.oilandgasin-quirer.com/article.asp?article=%5Cmagazine%5C071126%5Cmag2007%5Fnq0001%2Ehtml on May 12, 2009.

Carson Energy Services Ltd. website. Accessed via http://carson-welding.com on May 22, 2009.

Ross, Elsie. (January, 2009). Technology unlocks Bakken potential in Saskatchewan. *Heavy Oil and Oilsands.* [Electronic version]. Accessed via http://www.oilandgasinquirer.com/profiler.asp?article=%5Cprofiler%5C090112%5Cpro2009%5Fjc0002%2Ehtml on April 19, 2009.

Saskatchewan's top 100 companies 2008. *SaskBusiness Magazine.* [Electronic version]. Accessed via http://sasktop100.ca/ on August 26, 2009.

Saskatchewan's Top 100 Companies 2009. (2009). *SaskBusiness Magazine.* 30(6), 15-21.

Zinchuk, Brian. (March, 2009). Ron Carson – Big success from a small town. *Pipeline News.* p. B1-2.

End notes

1   The American Petroleum Institute gravity, or *API gravity*, is a measure of how heavy or light a petroleum liquid is compared to water. If its API gravity is greater than 10, it is lighter and

floats on water; if less than 10, it is heavier and sinks. Generally, oil with an API gravity between 40 and 45 commands the highest prices. Above 45 degrees the molecular chains become shorter and less valuable to refineries. Light crude oil is defined as having an API gravity higher than 31.1 °API.

2 Elsie Ross.

3 Mike Byfield.

4 Mike Byfield.

5 "Pigging" is jargon term describing a test for pipeline integrity.

6 SaskBusiness magazine.

Photo credits

All photos courtesy of Ron Carson and Carson Energy Services Ltd. private collections, except page 107. Page 107 illustration courtesy of Petrobakken Energy Ltd.

Chapter 11

Wayne Lorch
A legacy of invention

Interviews
Kathleen Lorch, Wayne Lorch.

Other sources

Friesen, (first name unknown). (year unknown).The Spy Hill story. [Booklet].

Grosse, N. (1999, January 27). Lorch snowplane eye-opener in 1930. *Ag World*. p. 9.

Johnstone, B. (1998, April 13). Immigrant funds dying, Lorch blames federal government. *Regina Leader-Post*, D1-2.

Johnstone, B. (1994, June 27). Program helps many, Saskatchewan-based funds raise $400M. *Regina Leader-Post*, D1-2.

Spy Hill High School Yearbook. (1956). Spy Hill, SK: Author.

Swedberg-Kohli, S. (June, 1984). 10 men to watch. *The Women's Guide*. p. 38.

The Lorch Snowplane Story. (1974). Wolverine Hobby and Historical Society. [Booklet]. Spy Hill, SK: Author.

End notes

1 Friesen.

2 From the family's collection of patent papers.

3 Karl Lorch. Introduction. The Lorch Snowplane Story. (1974).

4 New Development Flyer reprint. (1974). The Lorch Snowplane Story.

5 Spy Hill High School Yearbook.

6 IMC K1 & K2 were the names of the two mines.

7 A reference to a line from Kenneth Grahame's beloved classic, The Wind in the Willows. The complete line, which Ratty says to Mole, is: "There is nothing–absolutely nothing–half so much worth doing as simply messin' about in boats."

8 2006 Regina Chamber of Commerce "Paragon" Award.

9 2008 Regina Better Business Bureau "Torch" Award.

Photo credits

All photos courtesy of Lorch family private collection.

Chapter 12

George Reddekopp
Let's make a deal

Interviews
George Reddekopp, Rod Thiessen.

Photo credits

All photos courtesy of Reddekopp family and Grandwest private collections.

NOTES

Chapter 13

Gord & Cas Broda
Digging deep

Interviews
Cas Broda, Gord Broda.

Other sources

Big (rock & dirt) movers. (Spring, 2003.) *Western Forest Report*. 5(2), 21-24.

Celebrating 50 years. (2007, October 25). *The Saskatoon StarPhoenix*. [Supplement].

Hughes, Bob. (2004). The big dig: the miracle of Wascana Centre. (Regina: Leader Post).

Salgado, Brian. (October, 2005). Performing for the crowds. *Construction Today*.

End notes
1   Hughes, p. 10.
2   Hughes, p. 51.
3   Hughes, p. 54.

Photo credits
All photos courtesy of Broda family and Broda Group of Companies private collections.

Chapter 14

Bill & Irma Smith
The couple that really cooked

Interviews
Bill Smith, Irma Smith.

Other sources

What this country needs is more people like William and Irma Smith. [Advertisement]. (1984, February 28). *The Globe and Mail*. p. B5.

Six Seasons advertisement. (1992, November 14). *The Saskatoon StarPhoenix*. p. D13.

PKF Consulting website. Accessed via http://www.pkfc.com on August 14, 2009.

End notes
1   Haddock, Shirley. Personal correspondence, November 16, 1987.
2   Roynat press release, pg. 1, para. 3.
3   Roynat press release, pg. 2, para 2.
4   From Six Seasons advertisement.
5   PKF Consulting is a national firm of management consultants, industry specialists and appraisers who provide a full range of services to the hospitality, real estate and tourism industries.

Photo credits
All photos and illustrations courtesy of Bill & Irma Smith.

INDEX

INDEX

Italicised text refers to a caption.

INDEX